D1001744

EX LIBRIS

Pace
University
New York · Westchester

PACE PLAZA
NEW YORK

ARISTOTLE ON EQUALITY AND JUSTICE

By the same author

JOHN LOCKE: Essays on the Law of Nature
REMEMBERING: A Philosophical Problem
SEVENTEENTH-CENTURY METAPHYSICS
HOBBES AND LOCKE: The Politics of Freedom and Obligation

ARISTOTLE ON EQUALITY AND JUSTICE

His Political Argument

W. von Leyden

St. Martin's Press   New York

© W. von Leyden 1985

All rights reserved. For information, write:
St. Martin's Press, Inc., 175 Fifth Avenue, New York, NY 10010
Printed in Hong Kong
Published in the United Kingdom by The Macmillan Press Ltd.
First published in the United States of America in 1985

ISBN 0-312-04918-8

Library of Congress Cataloging in Publication Data
Leyden, W. von (Wolfgang von), 1911–
Aristotle on equality and justice.
Includes bibliographical references and index.
1. Aristotle–Political science.   2. Aristotle–Law.
3. Justice (Philosophy)   4. Equality–Philosophy.
5. Law–Philosophy.   I. Title.
B491.J87L48   1985   320'.01'1   85–1886
ISBN 0-312-04918-8

B
491
.J87
L48
1985

Contents

Preface

The issues chosen for examination in this book are central not only to Aristotelian doctrine, but to political philosophy in general and present-day discussion in particular.

For instance, there are those who argue for equality pure and simple without regard for the differences between human capacities and functions. Others, however, advocate preferential treatment for a minority irrespective of whether this is in the interest of the common good. Aristotle contends that, because of the absence of relevant resemblances and adequate criteria of comparison, it is difficult to establish true equalities between members of different social classes and individuals of diverse character and abilities. It follows that a more narrowly defined equality between men in one sphere may go together with a considerable variety of human potential and achievement elsewhere in the body politic. In particular, since equal shares would not always be fair, fair shares need not always be equal. One might then argue that only an unfair discrimination of *any* sort should be remedied and replaced by equal or at least just treatment, whether through legal means, public pressure or revolutionary action.

My choice of subject matter has been determined by a desire to contribute to the discussion of the Aristotelian as well as modern questions of (a) how to render the principle of equality, no less than that of inequality, compatible with the idea of fairness, and (b) how to combine the facts of individual as well as social diversity in civil life with the demands for political justice and cohesion.

Aristotle advances many illustrations and arguments, queries and conclusions, bearing on these issues. He reflects whether political rule should be in the hands of a few deserving people or in those of the general body of citizens. Sometimes he assumes that these two aspects of being meritorious and of having common characteristics are of equal importance. He also perceives that a state is composed not only of different elements but of different *kinds* of elements, and that this is necessarily so both in commercial dealings and in the contributions of citizens to the public good. For how could equality ever have become an issue if men had truly and clearly been equal, instead of different? This leads him to consider whether there are reliable criteria for grading men and the relative merits of their social functions and achievements. He leaves it unclear, however, whether his principle of proportionate equality, which largely insists on the factor of variety and difference, is to apply within any one area of employment only, or to all professional occupations throughout the whole of society. On the other hand, he stresses that such notions as desert, equality, justice and the public interest depend on interpretation and hence (one might say) on varying moral or political forms of understanding. Certainly, he is in no doubt that equalities assume different significance in different categories of discourse, and therefore also vary in meaning from one social class or 'part' of a state to another.

What most of these arguments have in common is an emphasis on a *contextual* interpretation of political theory and practice. This is a sensitive philosophical issue. The role which Aristotle assigns in the *Metaphysics* to such common terms as equality and inequality, especially in the context of his doctrine of categories, sets the stage for the introduction of purely formal concepts to his political theory. For 'equality' is a term which can be applied in metaphysical and political thought no less than in other fields of discourse, though it assumes a different meaning in each context. I believe that the ultimately logical arguments about equality in Aristotle's *Physics* (bringing to mind some of Russell's formulations on this topic) also have a bearing – in fact a much stricter one – on his discussion of equality and difference in the *Politics*. I have described both these findings in Chapter 2. This is followed in Chapter 3 by a detailed exegesis of those passages in the *Politics* which deal with the factor of difference in civil society.

Another part of Aristotle's political philosophy concerns the practice and theory of revolution and the rule of law, natural as well as conventional. These two areas of outstanding political interest, which I have investigated in Chapter 4, are of additional significance for Aristotle's arguments about a fair equality and the question of discrimination in society. There are also his exposition of the multiple meaning of law, and his insistence on the demands of equity. Again, he advances the possibility of various levels of interpretation in connection with the question of whether tradition or progress should influence the law-making process. Finally, an attempt is made to determine whether Aristotle's theory contains the rudiments of a doctrine of natural law. I have found it harder to ascertain whether his views on equality and justice, diversity and law, with all the subtle distinctions he draws, form a well-connected whole – an issue I examine in Chapter 5. However, I agree with Werner Jaeger's general assessment that the new and important feature in Aristotle's *Politics* is the union of normative thought with the ability to organise the multiplicity of actual political facts. In spite of this general recognition, I must stress that the examination of Aristotle's political doctrine throughout this book is entirely the result of my own interpretation.

In the last two sections of Chapter 4 use has been made of passages from my paper on 'Aristotle and the Concept of Law' in *Philosophy* (1967). Sincere thanks are due to the editor, Renford Bambrough, for permission to reproduce this material, though it appears here in a much revised and considerably expanded form. I am also indebted to Miss Mary Ryle for allowing me to include in this book quotations from a letter to me from Professor Gilbert Ryle.

Finally, my thanks are due to the London School of Economics and Political Science which, over the last five years, has given me an opportunity of testing this material in postgraduate classes, to the benefit of the author and, I hope, his advanced students.

W. von L.

London

1   Proportionate Equality and Social Class

(i) JUSTICE AND EQUALITY

In philosophy and political theory, perhaps more than in other fields of study, special attention is required for the discussion of certain key issues. On the one hand, there are concepts which cannot be adequately understood unless they are examined together with others which 'cluster' around them. An example is freedom, which has close connections with such notions as power, choice, voluntariness and right; or desire, which calls to mind wishes, wills, wants and appetites. On the other hand, there are concepts which are themselves polymorphous because of the multifarious use of the words denoting them. Apart from happiness, work or goodness, freedom itself is such an open-ended and variable concept, for the word may mean (among many other widely different senses) immunity, release, emancipation, permission, autonomy or licence. In order to prepare the ground and achieve clarity in an analysis of the two kinds of concept I have described (i.e. the one forming family ties with others, and the flexible, protean variety), it is important that their nature and function are understood at the outset.

The concepts of justice, equality and law (to which equity may be added) form a family in the sense indicated. In view of this complexity, it is difficult to deal with any one of these ideas independently of the others. For instance, we speak of 'equality before the law', 'justice under the law', or 'equity supplementing law'. The complication is increased by the fact that each of the terms mentioned in turn has several senses, so that, in attempting an analysis, it is essential to indicate precisely which, out of a range of possible meanings, one wishes to define.

For instance, in the case of justice, one would have to distinguish between commutative justice (the reason underlying the keeping of contracts or the exchange of goods), corrective justice (the infliction

1

of punishment on retributive, deterrent or reformatory grounds), juridical justice (the principle of equal treatment before the law), distributive justice (the idea of fairness in the dispensing of honours, offices, etc.), and the relation between conservative and reformative justice (i.e. the desirability of preserving the law as it stands or allowing it to develop). Having clarified the concept in this way, one can proceed to an analysis of, say, justice in the distributive sense, and interpret it as an equal treatment of equals, so that treating like cases differently or unequals equally must, according to this definition, be unjust.

But then – because of the overlapping of the two concepts – a criterion for equality is also called for. A recommendation frequently put forward is that a distribution of rewards is equal and hence just, if it is commensurate with the different abilities, merits or needs of people, or with each citizen's contribution to the public interest. An overriding stipulation is that an equal treatment of men should not be determined by such irrelevant factors as the colour of their skin.[1] What is involved here is the principle of equity (at least in one of its uses), in the light of which the notions of equality and justice must be redefined. Once this is done, the case for justice may be put by stating that equal treatment should be accorded to persons known to be equal in relevant respects, and unequal treatment to those known to be unequal in relevant respects. From here it is a short step to a consideration of the rule of law and the idea of equality before the law. Both principles involve reference to the concepts of equity and impartiality – the first with respect to judicial decisions by those who apply legal rules, the second in relation to the application of such rules to people in general. There is also an implicit appeal here to justice as a higher principle. In such an event, one's intention might be to refer either to the spirit, rather than the letter, of the law, or to ultimate standards of social justice.

One of the first to offer detailed arguments about justice, equality, equity and the law along the lines indicated was Aristotle.[2] He recognised that (a) these notions overlap in meaning and are thus interdependent; (b) justice is used in many senses;[3] (c) some proportion has to be introduced in defining the principle of 'distributive justice'; and (d) the concept of equity, particularly that of an equitable inequality between men, is indispensable for a proper discussion of justice, merit and the public interest. He also realised (though only within limits) that one is faced with considerable difficulty in attempting to apply the same criterion of equality to different professional or social classes. Moreover, in his opinion, questions of equality are frequently decided by either revolutionary or legislative means, and in the last analysis by reliance on principles of natural justice.

I shall consider each of these points in turn – particularly the problem which arises if claims to equality are assessed in relation to a plurality of social classes.

At times, Aristotle defined his views on equality with reference to his doctrine of distributive justice.[4] On these occasions, one could say that he regarded the concept of justice as essential to a satisfactory theory of social equality – a perfectly intelligible notion for anyone interested in values, since justice is a more obviously normative concept, both in the rational[5] and in the ethical sense, than equality (though this, as we shall see, has its own normative – logical as well as moral – undertones). On the other hand, it is also true that he wished to argue that principles of justice depend on a background of law and constitutional rule, and that these rely for their justification on the notion of equity and particularly on an adequate definition of equality before the law. On the latter basis, Aristotle viewed the concept of equality as being central to that of justice, whereas on the former he conceived of the idea of justice as central to that of equality. Though attention will be drawn to both views at various stages throughout this book, it is the evaluation of justice as a principle essential to an adequate theory of equality which I propose to consider now.[6] For Aristotle recognised that a truly defensible definition of equality depended on a compromise between the two doctrines of distributive justice prevalent in his day. One was the democrats' assertion that equality in respect of free birth, or that each man was to count for only one, represented the principal aspect of equality, and hence could be generalised so as to mean equality in any respect whatsoever. The other was the oligarchs' thesis that superiority in one respect (e.g. wealth, or nobility of birth) meant superiority on all counts.

Now Aristotle believed that the two principles of equality and superiority could be reconciled with each other if both were made amenable to the factor of justice, and particularly to that of equity. He considered that this could be achieved by his notion of 'proportionate equality'[7] – a notion, he hoped, acceptable to both sides in the dispute. What he had in mind was that each man should be awarded responsibilities as well as financial benefits in proportion to his deserts. For instance, as we might argue nowadays, a soldier who fights bravely and is mentioned in dispatches should have a greater claim to promotion or decoration than one who does not distinguish himself. Similarly, a competent teacher should draw a higher salary than an incompetent one, even though the latter might be his senior in years. Any person thus rewarded would receive an unequal share in the form of some preferential treatment; anyone not rewarded would be treated unequally in the sense of being passed over. In either case, the principle of proportionate equality prevails, for the *criterion* of treatment remains the same. With the ratio between desert and recognition remaining identical in all cases, some of the democrats' ideal of equality can obviously be preserved. On the other hand, with the criterion of a higher degree of both desert and reward resting on a man's superior skill or on his greater contribution to the well-being of the state, some of the oligarchs' ideal of preferential treatment can likewise survive. The advantage of Aristotle's doctrine is that it satisfies the demands of social justice in both aspects: the principle of proportionate equality is more equitable than the democrats' conception of mere numerical equality. Similarly, the idea of special privilege which his doctrine introduces is more justifiable than the oligarchs' claim that either wealth or noble birth by itself deserves the highest rewards.

There is one further merit in Aristotle's doctrine. His pronouncements on what should count as equal are not so vague[8] as other traditional examples. The thesis he advocates is theoretically clear as well as practical, whereas conventional egalitarian formulae are not only indeterminate but largely inapplicable. It should be acknowledged, however, that traditional principles of equality represent a moral *desideratum*, mainly perhaps as a result of their affinity with the commonsense idea of justice; they also have a strong appeal on aesthetic grounds, as can be seen from the variety of artistic norms relating to symmetry and regularity.[9] Nor can it be doubted that in a general sense there is something intuitively rational about the principle. Consider, for instance, Bentham's formula[10] that every man is to count for one, and no one for more than one; or the anecdote of the two sons who, because each expects at least an equal share of his father's inheritance, seize upon the idea that one of them (no matter which) should have the right to divide the legacy and that the other could then choose between the two halves. The idea of one party to a dispute dividing and the other choosing has, besides its general intellectual, also a practico-political appeal:

James Harrington introduced it in his *Oceana*[11] with reference to the two-chamber system.

It remains true, nevertheless, that the principle of equality, in any of its normal formulations, is abstract and vague. It is abstract, if not wholly inappropriate, when applied in situations which contain important differences. It is vague, if not altogether indeterminate in meaning, because it lacks a fixed rule for its use. Moreover, there are borderline cases where one is unable to say whether the word 'equality' does or does not apply. If this ambiguity becomes pervasive, any use of this word will become contestable. If the indeterminacy is such that the word does not express any concept at all, it could be said to be 'hopelessly vague',[12] in contradistinction to words of lesser degrees of vagueness. I do not think that a word such as 'equality' falls into this last category of hopelessly vague words. But, whatever the nature of either the vagueness or the generality of the word, it is probably because of these deficiencies that, as Harrington puts it, 'philosophers are disputing upon it in vain'.

In addition to being abstract and vague, the postulate of equality is tantalisingly empty. Consider the utilitarian formula that each man is to count for one and only one, or the socialist dictum that 'any and every human being has as much right as anyone else to whatever gives value to human life'.[13] Such pronouncements amount to Justinian's rule 'to each his own' *(suum cuique tribuere)*,[14] i.e. to some essentially fair adjustment of things in accordance with every man's due. However, in this bare form, the rule is a truism, particularly if it is intended to convey no more than that equals deserve equally and must be treated equally.[15] On the other hand, if the rule is meant to be informative, it suggests no more than the idea of some sort of order, purpose or uniformity: it leaves undetermined who, in any given case, is equal to whom, in which respects men are equal, what is every man's due, or what gives value to human life. If one were to ask what rationale the principle has, the answer might be that, on the basis of utilitarianism, there is none and that, if some ideology is to provide a rationale, there is no obligation to accept it.

The upshot of my discussion is that the common formulae of egalitarianism as pronounced by Bentham or Justinian are surrounded by limitations. Any principle which urges that similar cases should be accorded similar treatment is vague and empty precisely because it is incomplete. This is so with sentences containing the words 'similar' or 'free'[16] no less than with those containing the word 'equal'.[17] All these words seem fully descriptive. Yet to say 'A resembles B' is not to make a complete and truly informative statement, unless it is conveyed in what respect A and B resemble one another. Again, merely to say 'John is free' or 'The French are more free than the Russians' is to make incomplete statements. They become complete and informative only if it is stated that either John or the French are free (for example) from want, anxiety or legal restrictions, or that they are free to talk to friends and to travel abroad. Similarly, the egalitarian rule may be considered complete if it states in which respects men are to be 'counted for only one'. If this requirement is fulfilled, it will appear that the rule now embodies certain ends, interests and beliefs, which we consider legitimate and which we might wish to see conjoined with the 'counting for one' principle.

What Aristotle's notion of proportionate equality achieves is (a) to rid the egalitarian formula of its vagueness and incompleteness, and (b) to qualify it in the light of criteria taken from a wide scale of social purposes and attainments. The result is that equality ceases to mean sameness or uniformity, and instead the demands of merit, the public interest and equity all help to define the relevant grounds for treating some people equally and others differently.

(ii) THE RELATIONSHIP BETWEEN THE PRINCIPLES OF EQUALITY AND EQUITABLE INEQUALITY

This brings me back to the chief merit of Aristotle's doctrine. Instead of introducing the concept of equality plain and simple, whose application in a moral and in a political context is bound to suffer from the shortcomings I have mentioned, he prefers to indicate to what extent his notion of proportionate equality is grounded in the principle of a *fair* and *reasonable* inequality of treatment. In other words, rather than upholding the idea of a pervasive equality of men at all times and in all respects, he formulates criteria that *justify* certain inequalities between men. His reason for replacing the principle of equality by that of the justifiability of inequality was probably two-fold.

In the first place, the principle of equality is elusive: it arises from a wish rather than a fact, a judgement of value rather than a description of reality. Indeed, one might say that it is in the nature of a moral claim or demand, not unlike Rousseau's emphatic statement that man is born free,[18] which would seem to imply, if not to stipulate, that all men *ought* to be free. In Locke's *Second Treatise of Government*, the bifurcation between the factual and the normative on this issue is explicitly affirmed. In one passage[19] we read (as in Rousseau's pronouncement) that men are born free. In another,[20] Locke substitutes for this avowal the declaration that man is born, 'as has been proved', with a *title* to perfect freedom. In a similar way, Bentham's dictum 'every man to count for one' might be taken to express that every man has a right to or ought to count for one, or that he is meant to count for one. However, if the idea of a fundamental equality between all men represents a moral claim, it could be countered by the opposite claim – though hardly anyone would wish to go so far as Gladstone, in whose view 'equality was so utterly unattractive to the people of this country, inequality was so dear to their hearts'.[21] Still, that a fear of equality exists may be gathered from a sociological survey,[22] whose author observes 'that it is as important to explain why revolutions and radical social movements do *not* happen as it is to explain why they do'.

Secondly, even if the principle of equality does not describe facts and is more in the nature of a moral demand, it fails to be convincing. Though it figures in a general sense in almost all systems of ethics, it runs counter to the spirit of morality with its presupposition of men's different stations and functions, especially their obligations and duties of obedience on the one hand, and their rights and positions of authority on the other.[23] Examples are the preferential treatment accorded to parents, benefactors and persons to whom one has made a promise or bargained with, and the treatment involved in shunning the dishonest and punishing offenders. It is only if one thinks of a state outside ordinary morality that claims on behalf of a general equality between men may be found to be applicable. Hobbes argued[24] that, if one considered man's individual faculties of mind and body, all men must be pronounced equal. For their physical inequalities are outweighed by the possibility that the weaker may resort to secret machinations or the help of confederates; and, so far as wisdom is concerned, every man seems 'contented with his share'. Within the sphere of morality, on the other hand, it would be truer to say that the claim to equality is left vague, or else cannot be determined without the introduction of qualifications likely to militate against its *prima facie* plausibility. For, as I have shown, moral duties no less than moral rights involve inequalities, and these, rather than being unacceptable, are relevant, fair, and indeed essential.

Hence what needs explaining is not merely that in certain cases one might prefer one man to another, but that some preferences can be justified by means of identifiable and generally acceptable criteria. It should be stressed, however, that Aristotle's or any other philosopher's attempt to justify certain unequal measures in the treatment of men need not imply any strict anti-egalitarianism. There are people who hold, partly perhaps because they regard the concept of equality as vague and abstract, that no weight should be attached to it; that in fact there is no equality, never has been, and never will be. To my mind, this is a *non sequitur*. For, assuming that no men are either alike or treated equally, it is none the less obvious that no one, not even a thoroughgoing anti-egalitarian, would acquiesce in *any* unequal treatment, particularly of himself. Though he may say that there is no equality between men, he cannot say that reasons for unequal treatment are inadmissible, nor that these may all be founded on arbitrary decisions or irrational factors. But once he distinguishes between different kinds of unequal treatment, some that he can approve of and others that he cannot, he might have to concede that the claim to equality represents one of the validating criteria of inequality at some level or other, directly or indirectly. This admission takes the bottom out of the anti-egalitarian thesis. For if one approves of the preferential treatment accorded, say, to the deserving, one has to allow that their rewards should be proportionate to their talents or efforts, and indeed also to any losses incurred in the performance of their tasks. The same applies to cases in which people serving some public interest are given assistance or remunerative positions to further their work. Although here there is an explicit absence of consideration for other people, the promotion of public benefactors does not disregard the interests of the rest of the community; on the contrary, its whole justification is based on the principles of equality and the common good. For while the benefits derived from such enterprises as cancer research become public property and serve the general social interest, at the same time their equal distribution to those in need is fundamentally desirable and fair.

This brings me to another example of the observance of the principle of equality in a case of justifiable inequality, i.e. the granting of preferential treatment to people suffering from hardship. Here the validating conditions could be summed up in the formula 'to every one according to his needs'. The distribution of social security benefits is justifiable on these grounds, for while this treatment is seemingly unequal, it equalises the opportunities of the poor and the elderly with those of the better off and the young. It can be argued that the reason for this discrimination is the desire to restore to certain people equality of status with their fellow men – an equality they have forfeited by being either poor or old. Alternatively, one might say that the preferential treatment is an attempt to compensate the destitute and the old for disadvantages in their position – disadvantages for which they cannot be held responsible.[25]

My point, then (and I believe Aristotle's too), is that the principle of equality in the context discussed admits of a weak and of a strong form. In its weak aspect, it enjoins that men should never be treated differently in any respect without justification, that is, until relevant grounds for the discrimination have been advanced.[26] In its strong aspect, the principle prescribes not that men should be treated equally in all respects and at all times – which would indeed be impossible – but that they should never be treated differently in any respect, except in order to treat them equally in another, more 'fundamental' respect.[27] This strong definition, in my view (though I wonder whether in Aristotle's too), does not presuppose a belief in any universal property in men, in respect of which all are alike and equal. For the criterion by which all reasonable inequality of treatment is ultimately validated is not some generic equality which men must possess in order to count as men and as fundamentally equal, but merely some aspect of equality, which depends on the nature of the context, and accordingly varies from one of the types of justifiable inequality I have described to another.

This point helps to explain why the claim to equality, in spite of being vague and often unreasonable, has none the less survived and still forms part of moral and political discussion. Indeed, what the concept of equality stands to gain from a consideration of the various relevant types of inequality and from the question of their justification is the opportunity of weaning itself from its vagueness. The process of clarifying this concept by inquiring into the extent to which unequal forms of treatment are justifiable, forces into the open a number of illuminating issues.[28] These might concern the linguistic criteria which determine different senses of the words 'equality', 'inequality', 'equity' and the like, and also the correct use of these terms in their different senses. Alternatively, some factual information might emerge about conditions influencing the use of these words on a given occasion. By means of these and other recognised methods of inquiry, it should be possible to provide the principles I have discussed with a definite context – to the satisfaction of the egalitarian and the non-egalitarian alike (at least the more broad-minded amongst them). It would be a mistake, however, to expect such arguments to be simple, complete or final. After all, no kind of inquiry, be it philosophical or factual, scientific or non-scientific, provides answers which are of one piece, perfect, and in no need of revision.

On the other hand, if the claim to equality is not adequately specified and scrutinised, the egalitarian might be led to assert practically anything in defence of his cause. He might hold that it would be wrong to pay the unintelligent more than the intelligent, because society should compensate for the unhappiness which is the usual lot of the intelligent. He might say that the intelligent should not be paid more than the unintelligent, because society should compensate for genetic injustice. Again, he might affirm that it is wrong to pay people who enjoy their work as highly as those who do not.[29] A fanatical egalitarian might argue that the inequality of the members of a football team in relation to their captain is such that it is better to have no football played at all than to have it played by a team led by a captain. Or consider Lord Lindsay's example of a tutorial class he supervised, which indignantly repudiated as undemocratic an examination in which some passed and others failed. The example is an expression of the literal democratic temper which rejects standards of excellence and equalises by downgrading.[30] This defence of the claim to equality is not only arid but unprincipled. On the whole, people have come to agree that the interests of both equality and justice are best served if the most capable candidates fill the key posts, and if people with expertise exercise authority. Indeed, it may be argued that the best way in which to eliminate real injustice is to secure acceptance of all justifiable inequality between men. For, as Aristotle said, injustice arises as much from treating unequals equally as from treating equals unequally.

(iii) JUSTICE AND EQUALITY IN THE EXCHANGE OF GOODS: THE ANALOGY OF BUILDERS AND SHOEMAKERS

Aristotle's theory of proportionate equality, in which the principle of equality is combined with that of equitable inequality, can be applied in a variety of ways, some of which raise no difficulties, while others are to a greater or lesser extent problematic. Its most obvious use is within any one trade or profession, e.g. builders, shoe-makers, farmers, soldiers or teachers. That is, efficient teachers should receive a greater reward for their work (i.e. in terms of remuneration and promotion) than should inefficient ones. A simi-lar line of treatment would apply to soldiers or administrators, and so on, respectively.

The grounds for this restricted principle of distributive justice are relatively straightforward. Preferential treatment ought to be accorded to all teachers (or soldiers, administrators, and the like) meriting it, in such a way that the magnitude of the reward is correl-ated with the degree of desert in an ascending scale. Correspond-ingly, the less deserving should obtain less favourable treatment, and the least deserving the smallest reward. In these circumstances, two equally efficient teachers would receive an equally high reward, and two equally inefficient ones an equally low one. And while those who deserve alike will be treated equally (i.e. either favourably or unfavourably, as the case may be), those whose merits and achievements differ will be treated unequally (i.e. a teacher of excel-lence will receive greater recognition than a mediocre one, and a mediocre teacher greater recognition than an incompetent one). One can think of further modifications in this method of apportion-ing different degrees of recognition to different degrees of achieve-ment. For instance, one might treat an efficient (though junior) teacher on equal terms with a senior and more experienced (though less efficient) one, or on better terms, or on less favourable ones. The criterion of treatment in the three cases would depend on the value one sets on such factors as age, experience and efficiency. Most disputes involving comparability can be settled fairly readily, once their premises and the contexts in which they arise are agreed upon, or once the objectives of a given profession and the criteria for assessing the worth of its members and their service are clarified.

The point at issue is that in some sense or other, it is possible to draw comparisons between, say, efficiency and advanced age, junior status and experience, or between a versatile method of approach and maturity. On such a basis, one might assess the flexibility and imaginative nature of approach on the part of a relatively unknown teacher as being of equal value to the mature status of a long-established one. If there is agreement on points of this nature, then there should be no difficulty in the distribution of equal awards to people who, though in one sense noticeably different, can in another more relevant sense be considered alike.

Problems arise if comparisons are made between trades or professions which are significantly different. In this case, the principle of proportionate equality might either find a limit to its application, or have to be qualified so as to be comprehensible in a broader sense. If the problem is to establish comparisons between a builder and a shoemaker, correlations between the achievements of these men and their rewards might be considered feasible. The principle of proportionate equality could then be applied to the extent that one would remunerate a reliable builder and a reliable shoemaker on equal terms, but treat a first-rate builder and a second-rate shoemaker differently. What the principle would stipulate in general is that the emoluments or status of builders, shoemakers, and the like should be proportional to their deserts, and that the ratio between reward and desert should be the same not only for all individual cases *within each* of these groups, but also – and more importantly – *throughout* these various trades.

I shall now deal in detail with this wider application of the principle, reserving until later the more problematic case of comparing the merits, and hence the rewards, of reliable shoemakers, first-rate farmers, efficient teachers, top-ranking officers, successful doctors, and leading civil servants, i.e. pre-eminent members of a variety of trades and professions whose standing in the estimation of society is usually regarded as widely different.

The reason why comparisons within one given kind of employment are feasible is that the employees in question resemble each other in their training and abilities. Even comparisons between a skilful junior teacher and a not so efficient, though more experienced, senior master are possible because both are of the same profession and resemble each other in relevant respects. The case is similar with two different species of delphiniums, whose conforming characteristics enable a connoisseur to draw comparisons between them and to grade them according to one and the same standard. This principle holds true of members of any class resembling each other in respect of qualities they all share to a greater or lesser degree, be the class that of Italian Baroque architects, greyhounds or Jaffa oranges.

It is rather different with classes whose members do not resemble each other sufficiently, or where the respects in which they may be evaluated are not necessarily alike. This is the case with such larger classes as artists in general, or tradesmen taken as a whole.[31] In his *Nicomachean Ethics*, Book V, Aristotle illustrates the principles of distributive justice and proportionate equality by means of a comparison between a builder and a shoemaker, and subsequently between a farmer and a shoemaker: let us investigate the nature and rationale of such a comparison.

Aristotle starts from the assumption that justice or the just (in what he takes to be its 'particular' meaning) concerns either the distribution of honour, wealth and things like public offices which are shared among members of a political community, or the corrective just in the various voluntary transactions between one man and another. He also observes that the just, in its capacity of being the equal, is a mean and that, since the equal implies at least two terms or persons, and the mean is between two things (i.e. the greater or less), the just must imply at least four terms – two people to whom it is just and two things between which it is equal, or a mean. Hence the just consists of a proportion, geometrical in the case of distributive justice, arithmetical in that of rectificatory justice. In the case of distributive justice (and it is this with which we are concerned here), the proportion is that of the whole being to the whole as each part is to each part. In other words, of two men, A and B, A stands to his share C of the good distributed as B stands to his share D. A and B will then be in some sense equal, and so will be C and D.[32] The sense of the equality and hence of the equality of ratios would be determined according to some standard, though – as we have seen – ancient democrats and oligarchs differed over what that standard was, democrats being for freedom and oligarchs for wealth, just as some aristocrats would have opted for virtue, and others for nobility of birth. But whatever the standard may be, the general assumption is that, if persons are to be equal, they must have equal shares, and if they are not to be equal, they must have unequal shares. Controversion of this principle amounts to injustice. The formula concerning proportionate equality is thus A:B :: C:D (or A/B = C/D), and *permutando* A:C :: B:D, or A+C:B+D :: A:B.

Any of these formulae represents a process of equalisation between people who are different; it also suggests what portion each person should receive according to the standard of merit or justice. In Aristotle's example of the relation between a builder and a shoemaker, equalisation does not hold between these men as human beings or in their own right (for each may be in many respects sufficiently different from the other to exclude comparison), nor between their contributions to the true interests of society (for each contribution may be assessed by different standards). Instead, what Aristotle proposes is the notion of reciprocation,[33] not in the sense of 'an eye for an eye', as in the context of corrective justice, but in the form of dealings of exchange, as in the context of distributive justice. The reciprocation he has in mind is, as before,[34] in terms of proportion and exact equality, for, as he puts it, it is by mutual and proportionate contributions that a social community is held together.[35] None the less, the goods to be exchanged have to be equalised before dealings can begin. And here points of quality as well as quantity have to be considered, for if the builder's house is not as good as the shoemaker's boots, neither equality nor a just exchange can be achieved. That equality can be secured only if the goods are first equalised is also clear from the facts that (a) the producers of these wares are *ex hypothesi* different, and (b) no exchange arises between producers of the same kind, e.g. between two shoemakers or two physicians. Hence builder and shoemaker, though themselves different and unequal, are equalised by means of some comparable quality as well as quantity of their goods.

The calculation of an equal deal proceeds on the premises that (a) there must be reciprocation of action according to proportion, and (b) before reciprocation is attempted, there must be the same ratio between the wares as between the persons, i.e. the ratio of equality. Hence the same formula applies here as before, i.e. $A/B = C/D$.[36] Now, if the value of 100 pairs of (good) shoes is agreed to equal that of one (well-built) house, the shoemaker could be considered equal to the builder if he exchanges his 100 pairs of (good) shoes for the one (well-built) house. He would be not equal to the builder, but better off, if he exchanged 10 pairs of his shoes for the one house, and he would also be unequal, but worse off, if he exchanged 1000 pairs of shoes for the one house.

However, as Aristotle points out,[37] both money and demand are factors to be taken into account. In order to exchange wares, they have to be compared, and for the purpose of comparison one has to have a kind of medium, or some one measure of the wares in question. Money determines how many shoes are equal to a house, for if the same price is set on 100 pairs of (good) shoes as on one (well-built) house, the quantity no less than the value of these two wares is equal. If $x = £1000$, and a house costs $\frac{1}{2}x$ while a pair of shoes is worth $\frac{1}{200}$ of x, it is clear how many pairs of shoes are equal to one house, i.e. 100. However, money has no independent value: it is (a) liable to depreciation, (b) dependent on convention, and (c) representative of demand, which fluctuates. If there is little demand for houses, a shoemaker should be able to exchange, say, 10 pairs of shoes for one house, though without being better off in consequence; if houses are in great demand, he would have to exchange as many as, say, 1000 pairs of shoes for the one house, though again without being worse off as a result of this deal. In the former case 10 pairs of shoes, in the latter 1000 pairs, would be considered equal to one house. If houses are in no demand whatsoever, or the shoemaker is in no need of one, no exchange with the builder's wares takes place; nor, of course, will there be any exchange if neither of them wants the other's wares. But the greater the shoemaker's demand for a house, the lower the price commanded by his own products in exchange for one; and, correspondingly, the less he needs a house, the higher the price commanded by his shoes in such an exchange.[38]

It follows that, in spite of the fluctuations of demand and of the purchasing power of money, and despite the difference between building, shoemaking or farming, any one of these trades can be compared, equalised, and made proportionate to the others. The reason is that demand brings men together in transactions, varying inversely with the price obtained. On this basis, then, all things become commensurable and available for exchange.

One should not lose sight of Aristotle's admission that, before any exchange or dealing *(koinōnia)* can take place, a process of equalisation must be achieved, and that this is 'between people who are *different* and *unequal*',[39] as are builders, shoemakers or farmers. He also emphasises that, in spite of the fact that money is capable of rendering things commensurate, strictly speaking it is impossible that such dissimilar objects as houses and shoes should be commensurate, though with reference to demand they may become so.[40] Here the division of labour, the mutual dependence of crafts or trades, and the correspondence of supply and demand are well stated. But, as one commentator notes, 'it is a pity that these principles were not further carried out'.[41] The question at issue is how people can reach an agreement over the exchange value of their goods, if deception is to be excluded and interested parties do not exchange their goods in random amounts, nor set an unduly high value on those they part with and an unduly low one on those they receive.[42] Even if each trader sets a value both on his own and on another's wares before the exchange, are these values to be determined by (a) the quality of the labour spent, (b) the quantity, (c) the time expended in the production of the goods, or (d) the productivity, i.e. the rate of production of goods of unit value? As we have seen, the issue is even more complex in that the excellence of work (i.e. both its quality and its quantity) will have to be measured by the relation between supply and demand. Besides, Aristotle's view that the efficiency of a builder and that of a shoemaker can be compared and made commensurable with each other may give rise to the notion that the equal value of their products and the equal quality of the labour spent upon them shows that the excellence and productivity of the two men is identical – an unwarranted assumption. Above all, the correlation becomes less obvious if for the builder we substitute a world-famous conductor and for the shoemaker a minister of state. How can Aristotle's consideration apply in this new situation?

Similar questions arise if builders, shoemakers and farmers are compared not on the basis of the exchange value of their goods, but with reference to the quantity and quality of their contribution to the public welfare. With this type of inquiry we are reverting to the analysis of the principle of proportionate equality as applied to various trades and with regard to the ratio between their merits and rewards in the *whole* social context. What is at issue here is whether men's achievements in separate professional careers can be evaluated in comparison with one another, if comparisons in their mutual dealings already cause difficulties. People's opinions may vary about the value to be set on a bumper crop of potatoes compared with one of wheat, or on how to assess the latter in comparison with a maximum output of houses. Sometimes they may prefer houses, even inferior ones, to an adequate supply of food, or conversely, a small ration of food to the ownership of a house, even a palatial one. Differences of appraisal will be more pronounced when it comes to deciding which kind of goods contributes more to the public interest – food, housing, clothing, medical care or education. Whenever the relative merits of such goods are at issue, two questions have to be considered over and above the rest, i.e. firstly the degree or kind of difference involved, and how much stress to lay on it, and secondly the nature of any comparisons or equalities, and what emphasis to lay on that. I shall begin with the points relating to difference, leaving until later the question of equality.

(iv) ARISTOTLE'S EMPHASIS ON DIFFERENCE: THE CLAIMS OF DEMOCRACY VERSUS RULE BY EXPERTS

The best way in which to discuss Aristotle's views on the differences between people is to subdivide the investigation into two separate issues – the first dealing with the relations between various *trades* such as builders, shoemakers or farmers, and the second with the relations between various social *classes* such as the rich and the poor, or the high-born and the low- (though free-) born. Aristotle allows these two issues to merge,[43] a fact that is revealing if one wishes to argue, as I do, that for him there are differences in connection with the one issue just as much as there are in connection with the other. For purposes of analysis, I shall discuss the two issues separately.

First then, what has Aristotle to say about the relations between builders, shoemakers or farmers? One of the passages where he raises this question constitutes a critique of Plato.[44] In his own enumeration of the essential parts of a state, Aristotle mentions farmers, skilled mechanics, merchants, retailers, agricultural labourers,[45] and those making up the defence forces. Before continuing his enumeration, he points to three inadequacies in Plato's account. The first is that Plato regarded weavers, farmers, shoemakers and builders as the most necessary elements in his 'first state' (i.e. the first sketch of the city-state in *Republic*, Book II), and that, only because all these workers lack self-sufficiency, he added others such as smiths, herdsmen, merchants and retailers. Plato's second shortcoming, according to Aristotle, is the assumption that every state is formed for the supply of the necessities of human life, 'and not rather to achieve the Good'. His third criticism is that Plato considered shoemakers as indispensable as farmers.

In what sense, then, do Aristotle's criticisms of Plato imply an emphasis on the differences between trades as well as between social classes? His first two exceptions make it clear that Plato not only omits from his account certain sections of a state, but fails to recognise that the ones he does mention are less essential than those that would help achieve the Good. The purpose of his third point against Plato is to make a case for differentiating between shoemakers and farmers, and for accepting the latter as the more important of the two. This argument is repeated by Aristotle elsewhere in the *Politics*, for instance when he distinguishes between four varieties of democracy and claims that the best is one in which the common people are graded in such a way that farmers are at the top of the scale.[46] He explains subsequently[47] that 'none of the occupations followed by a populace consisting of mechanics, shopkeepers, and day labourers leaves any room for excellence'. This issue will be more fully explored at a later stage of my argument.

Let us return to Aristotle's enumeration of the necessary parts of the state. After listing the inadequacies of Plato's account, he goes on to assert that among the elements forming a political association, there must be an office for the dispensing of justice. In order to emphasise this point, he compares the relation between the state's spiritual requirements and its material needs with that between the mind and the body. Since, in his view, the mind is more essentially part of a living being than the body, he infers from this analogy that the contribution to the state's spiritual welfare is more valuable than that which serves its bodily needs.[48] The parts of a state which serve its spiritual well-being, he considers, are (a) the military (which he has already referred to in Section 10 as the fifth element in the constitution of a state), and (b) the administration of justice, together with the deliberative function of government. If (b) is reckoned as one element, Aristotle has now accounted for six necessary parts of the state. The sixth is again mentioned shortly afterwards (sect. 17), where it is emphasised that the judicial and deliberative functions are essential to all states and that, in order for them to serve the Good, they must be performed by men of ability. Aristotle lists two more parts of the state, thus making eight altogether. They are the rich, who sustain the state with their property, and magistrates, who discharge the executive duties of government. So far, then, we have encountered two attempts on Aristotle's part to grade the types of citizen that make up a state. He considers farmers more essential than shoemakers, and he values the army, the judiciary and men in public office more highly than those who attend to the physical needs of the community.

It is here that Aristotle introduces the second issue – that concerning the differences between social *classes*. He links this with the topic of his previous discussion by considering the classes of the rich and the poor as *parts* of a state. Since he has already mentioned the rich as the one preceding the eighth, the poor would be the ninth. He admits that there is something special about these two classes. Functions attached to the other parts of the state can be carried out by one and the same person: for instance, a man may be a soldier and a farmer; another both a judge and a member of the deliberative assembly. However, the same person cannot be simultaneously rich and poor. From this it follows (a) that these two classes are truly opposites; (b) that the most obvious division of every state is into these two; and (c) that either class can (according to which prevails) form a state, i.e. an oligarchy or a democracy.

Aristotle's distinction between these two constitutions is not just one between opposites, nor a distinction based on numbers, but one between *qualitative* characteristics. He explains this in the opening sections of the *Politics*, Book IV, Chapter 4, and in Book III, Chapters 6 and 8. In the former passage, he argues that a wealthy majority which excludes a poor, though free-born, minority from office is no democracy, any more than a poor but strong minority which prevents a rich majority from sharing office is an oligarchy. At the same time, he dissociates the concepts of democracy and oligarchy from the criterion of mere number by arguing that the distribution of offices on the basis of stature (as in Ethiopia) does not constitute an oligarchy, even though the number of tall men is invariably small. He concludes that a proper distinction between constitutions must be based on criteria additional to those of social position and mere number.

Aristotle himself provides a fuller analysis in the two earlier chapters already mentioned. There he starts from the assumption that the nature of a constitution depends, in the first place, on the idea of citizenship and on a principle determining the participation in deliberative or judicial office. In Book III, Chapter 6, he specifies a second criterion, namely the principle regulating the organisation of a state, especially the office of the supreme authority. The principle he has in mind is that which establishes the form of a state, and this for him is inextricably linked with that part of the civic body which holds supreme power. Thus in a democratic state the whole people are sovereign; in an oligarchy, the few privileged. The third criterion[49] which Aristotle advances for differentiating between constitutions is the nature of the end pursued by different states. This criterion is closely related to the fourth – the nature of political rule and of its holders. The reason for the connection is that, as Aristotle sees it, the true end of a state is always directed towards the good life – which is tantamount to the common good – and so the right kind of authority is that exercised in the common interest. The two criteria he suggests help to mark off not different constitutions as such, but two main *classes* of constitution, to which all particular constitutions can be assigned. He labels constitutions directed to the common good as 'right' or 'normal', those directed to the personal interest of rulers 'wrong' or 'perverted'.

Though the classification of constitutions into right and wrong is not one I wish to pursue, it should be noted that by implication it helps to distinguish between different 'right' constitutions. In referring to the variety of ends pursued by states as one of the bases for classifying constitutions, Aristotle conceives only of a qualitative, but distinctly ethical criterion. This is made more evident by his insistence that political rule is fundamentally for the benefit of the ruled, and that this specific utilitarian principle is 'the standard of absolute justice'.[50] One would expect that, if consideration of the common interest on the part of all those holding political power is to be the standard of absolute justice, each 'right' constitution should provide some definite illustration of this standard. Aristotle, however, remarks that 'the same laws cannot be equally beneficial to all oligarchies or to all democracies'.[51] From this argument it follows that the ethical criterion which differentiates between 'right' constitutions is the nature of the laws appropriate to each. The point is further demonstrated in the *Politics*, Book III, Chapter 9, where (as we have seen) Aristotle affirms that the principle of each constitution lies in its particular conception of justice, and that this is therefore also the ground for the basic difference between oligarchy and democracy.

Aristotle's last qualitative distinction between democracy and oligarchy is the one from which I started, that democracy is the rule of the poor (rather than the many) and oligarchy that of the rich (rather than the few). He considers this criterion essential, and the factor of number purely contingent.[52] In the chapters where he deals with this difference,[53] he explains that the central criterion is one of *social class*, which in the case of a democracy implies not only the poor but the free-born, and in that of an oligarchy not only the better-off but the nobler-born. It is clear that this criterion is a truly qualitative one; and, as one commentator puts it, 'in this insistence on the qualitative element Aristotle was pointing to a truth of real importance'.[54] Admittedly, the truth in question has no direct significance for present-day classificatory theory, for it is valueless in this respect.[55] None the less, it embodies the important recognition that the constitution of a state has its roots in (what in modern times has been called) its 'social system' or its 'form of life'. Moreover, if rich and poor coexist in a given state as two different classes, each will consist of separate social elements and have its own aims and functions, its own dominant character, and its own ethical view of life.[56]

The last point is by no means Aristotle's final word on the differences between the parts of a state. For instance, in Book IV, Chapters 14–16, he traces the variations between constitutions to the different deliberative, magisterial and judicial powers in each. In Book VI, Chapter 1, he draws attention to possible combinations of these three powers, in that constitutions may give rise to 'mixed' forms, each with a different 'balance' of power.[57] Books VI and VIII contain further reasons for constitutional variation, among them territorial characteristics and the circumstances of history. Talking of citizenship,[58] Aristotle reiterates his conviction that a state is composed of disparate elements and capacities, and that therefore 'there cannot be a single excellence common to all citizens, any more than there can be a single excellence common to the leader of a dramatic chorus and his assistants'.[59] His point is that the concept of a good citizen admits of various forms of excellence;[60] that, instead of defining this quality in general terms, one ought to enumerate the particular forms it takes in, say, women, men, parents, children, slaves, rulers, artisans and other specific trades. He continues the argument by maintaining that the excellence of citizens is relative not only to a given constitution, but also to the different stations and offices within a state. Elsewhere,[61] he remarks that some men (i.e. slaves, mechanics and labourers) are necessary conditions of a state, without always being integral parts of a civil community in the sense of sharing in the public administration. From this he concludes that just as there are various constitutions, so there are various kinds of members of a body politic: in one, mechanics and labourers are citizens; in another, not.

The status of farmers casts an interesting light on Aristotle's conception of the difference of kind[62] between peoples of different states. In one passage[63] he considers that, if the populace of one democratic state consists of farmers and that of another of mechanics and day-labourers, the two democracies differ. The reason for the distinction, as Aristotle sees it,[64] is a difference of *character*: where peasant farmers are sovereign, the people in charge of the government are of moderate means, they have to live by their work, and they are unable to enjoy any leisure. Since this group cannot devote much time to politics and has to confine meetings of the deliberative assembly to a minimum, it relies instead on the rule of law, which is made supreme. Of the four forms of democracy (which Aristotle distinguishes), this peasant form is both logically and chronologically the 'first'.[65] The 'last' is the extreme form, comprising mechanics and day-labourers. Characteristic features of this radical democracy are (a) an increased population, and (b) a corresponding increase in public revenue. It follows that, owing to a system of state-payment,[66] large numbers of people can join in political activity, and also that leisure facilities are now available for the enlarged lower classes, including the poor. Because of the frequency of popular meetings, the ordinary people (rather than the law) will become sovereign.[67]

This, then, is the backbone of Aristotle's classification of the four kinds of democracy.[68] The first, i.e. the agricultural, is considered to be the best, which explains (as we have seen) why he criticises Plato for ranking farmers equal to shoemakers. In Book VI, Chapter 4 of the *Politics*, Aristotle advances further reasons for his preference for an agrarian democracy: it ensures (a) a system of balance, (b) a sense of responsibility, and (c) government conducted by men of quality. In his opinion, a peasant population, excelling as it does in vigour and robust physique, has the additional advantage of making good soldiers. The people which form the three other varieties of democracy are, in Aristotle's view, of a much poorer stamp. As he points out, none of the occupations embraced by mechanics, shopkeepers and day-labourers leaves room for excellence of any sort. In fact, he argues, the mob that lives round the market-place tends to disturb the balance of a constitution. He therefore believes that, where citizens of no distinction share in every part of the administration (as in the extreme form of democracy), a policy of 'living as you like' is bound to find general support. Connivance at this practice, he concludes, must lead to the rise of demagogues, who in turn will promote the cause of either revolution or tyranny.[69]

Finally, some account should be taken of Aristotle's attempt to associate the differences between democracy and oligarchy with the different policies and qualifications of the parties representing these systems of government. The parties in question are the general body of citizens on the one hand, and the 'better sort of men'[70] (i.e. a privileged minority or persons with professional skills) on the other. As Aristotle indicates,[71] these competing groups always live *together* in every single state, and their claims are therefore *simultaneously present* under any constitution. It follows that the social policies and practices of one group live side by side with the political ideas and pressures of the other. For Aristotle, the issue is still one of distributive justice:[72] who should receive supreme recognition and be awarded with the highest office – the government of a state. But although only one party can rule at a given time, there will be at all times two opposite influences in a state:[73] one working towards rule by the people at large, and the other in the interests of the Few – whether they be the wealthy, some other privileged group, or men with special administrative skills.

What, then, are Aristotle's arguments on behalf of each of these rival claimants for supremacy in the state?[74] Clearly, the group defending the rights of the general population or at least of some popular body would extol the principles of democracy and equality. It would also advocate the view that the voice of the people *(vox populi)* is irresistible and irreducible, besides being wise and reliable. On the other hand, those who argue for a single ruler, or at most for a selected few, rely upon the superior abilities of experts, and approve of the special privileges bestowed on 'governors by profession'.[75] Now, Aristotle agrees with the first group, that the people as a whole have a combination of qualities that enables them to deliberate wisely[76] and to be better judges than specialists.[77] Hence he shares the opinion of those who plead that a popular assembly should exercise judicial functions, elect magistrates and scrutinise their conduct at the end of their tenure. One particular reason for his view is that the general body of citizens knows best 'how the shoe pinches'[78] and how much the ordinary man is prepared to suffer. As he puts it, the diner rather than the cook may be the best judge of a meal, just as a householder may know more about the usefulness of a house than either its builder or its architect.[79]

As opposed to claims by the people generally, Aristotle also sees some justice in those made on behalf of the most able. In some sense, he argues, persons with special training are better judges and possibly even better citizens than the amateur; it would therefore be wrong to grant political authority to a large number of ordinary men rather than to persons with professional skills. Aristotle offers no answer to the argument about 'shoes pinching', though it could be maintained that, even if the common man knows whether or how his shoe pinches, only the expert has the answer to where or why it pinches, and what the remedies are. Besides, if it is admitted that there are matters too complex to be fully understood by ordinary men, for instance economics or foreign affairs, and that there are forms of organisation (such as the Army or Navy) which, in order to be efficient, must of necessity be under autocratic control, the prin-

ciple that only those with technical knowledge should rule gains in
validity.

However, turning again to his original argument about the efficiency of popular assemblies, Aristotle remarks that the rule of the
Many secures impartiality and thus the rule of law.[80] He qualifies
this point by the consideration that, since it is impossible for all citizens to govern together at any given time, each should in turn participate in the functions of the governing assembly. But then, he
reflects, rule in the hands of one man or of the few eminent has the
quality of personal initiative; moreover, matters of detail are settled
more adequately by specialists. One could add to this argument the
observation that in a modern state, including local government, it is
impossible for every citizen to be a member of the deliberative body;
also that, if committees with a wide range of representatives from
the civic body are set up, it is unlikely that their decisions will be
rapid or their actions necessarily efficient.

One further point in favour of Aristotle's argument about popular
rule is that the majority of members of the civic body are adult,
rational and politically-minded persons; most of them have
common sense, and can gain political practice by training and
experience. Hence one might demand that the people at large
should be given political power and use it fully, thereby acquiring
further skills and a greater measure of responsibility. However, this
argument cannot be used as proof that the Many are collectively
superior to the Few. Indeed, it might be said that only members of
the upper classes are politically-minded, and that the capacity for
sound and informed judgement is not distributed evenly among all
layers of society. If, as is the case in democracies, large masses of
men are to be consulted about public affairs or questions concerning
technical development, these issues must first be made intelligible to
them – a procedure involving inadequate forms of presentation and
clear proof of the superiority of experts. In the opinion of students of
crowd mentality from Thucydides to Le Bon and Trotter,[81] the
masses are short-sighted, selfish, weak and suggestible: to let them
exercise political power would be unrealistic, even hazardous.

One final argument underlying the claims of the Many and the
Few concentrates on reasons for and against a plebiscite or referendum.[82] Aristotle is silent on this point, though the issue falls square-
ly within the confines of his discussion. For those who advocate the
principle of the sovereignty of the whole body of citizens plead for
their participation in all deliberative functions and for their decision

on important political questions by a direct general vote. The idea behind such plebiscites is that public issues are sometimes sufficiently straightforward to be formulated in a single question which can be answered by a single 'yes' or 'no'. Those who doubt the wisdom of seeking the views of the entire populace on a definite political question have advanced a variety of objections.[83] First, it is argued, one can never be sure whether voting is on the specific issue before the public or on their opinion of the politicians who contest it. Secondly, it is held that popular beliefs in political issues are often prejudiced and emotional rather than rational and informed. Finally, there is the widespread conviction that in a representative democracy such as Great Britain, a referendum would by-pass the parliamentary mechanism, diminishing the sense of responsibility in the representative body as well as disrupting the efficiency of government. Here again, two policies, two ideals, conflict. Advocates of a plebiscitary democracy (such as exists in Switzerland) will inevitably coexist in the same community with those who favour minority decisions. And there will always be, just as in Aristotle's city state, two opposing parties, one arguing that all policy-making must be confined to the experts, the other asserting that all administrative control should be a special function of the people.

This analysis of two main lines of reasoning in the debate about the seat and legitimacy of political power concludes my account of Aristotle's distinctions between the various parts of a state and between the different kinds of constitution. What matters to him throughout his study of civil society is the correct delineation of qualitative differences and differentiations in value. And even though, in his view, a state is a form of fellowship or 'communion' (*koinōnia*) united by a common aim and by common action, it is at the same time composed of dissimilar members, distinct functions and policies, and above all of diverse modes of life and excellence.[84]

2 Two Definitions of Equality and their Significance for Political Theory

(i) THE STRICT DEFINITION IN THE *PHYSICS*: KINDS AND SPECIES

We have reached a point where the application of the concept of equality to the members, functions and parts of a state, as viewed by Aristotle, becomes increasingly problematic. There may be a case for his doctrine of proportionate equality in connection with an assessment of the different achievements of farmers and, apart from this, in relation to the accomplishments of shoemakers, builders or generals, respectively. Perhaps, as we have seen, some basis for an equal deal can be established on the basis of the exchange rates for the wares of builders, shoemakers and farmers, alike. But then Aristotle differentiates sharply between farmers and shoemakers in his wider estimate of the functions and merits of different trades and classes in a state. Hence the question arises: how can the notion of equality be in any way employed in a context consisting of so much diversity, of both quality and value?

The issue becomes more complicated by the fact that equality can be defined in such precise and technically restricted terms as to be almost totally inapplicable to the subject matter of politics. Aristotle himself attempts to achieve this in his *Physics*,[1] where he asks what conditions must be satisfied for two changes, two quantities or two qualities (respectively) to be comparable and pronounced equal. The following are his main points, interspersed with illustrations and comments of my own.

First, a change in one thing and the locomotion of another cannot

26

be compared, even though both take the same time. For instance, if within twenty-four hours milk turns sour and a journey is completed, the two forms of change do not extend over the same sort of line or track and therefore cannot be said to move with equal velocity. Again, owing to the absence of a common measure, no circular motion can be compared with rectilinear motion, nor can a man turn back in his walk or go straight ahead with equal velocity. In the next place, the ambiguity of certain terms or the different context in which they are applied makes a comparison between two or more objects impossible, even if they are characterised by the same word. Thus sharp wine cannot be held equal to a sharp knife or a sharp tongue, nor can one say of a snail that it moves more slowly than a kettle boils or faster than a child develops. Similarly, 'much' earth does not mean the same as 'much' pleasure or 'much' strength, for these things differ in their nature and cannot be compared even with regard to volume. 'Equal' (or 'the same amount') is ambiguous too, and since 'equal' means the ratio of one to one, 'one' (or 'the one') may be considered ambiguous as well,[2] for whenever this phrase is used a critic might ask 'one what?' (or 'the one what?'). Hence 'one' note is not equal to 'one' tooth or 'one' nation, nor do the three add up to 'three' in the same sense.

Aristotle's discussion of equality is misleading here. 'Much' is defined by him as 'so much and more';[3] it thus means the same as the term 'magnitude', which Russell defines as 'anything which is greater or less than something else'.[4] This capacity for being greater or less, however, must not be associated, as it is by Aristotle, with the meaning of equality. As Russell explains, 'what can be greater or less than some term, can never be equal to any term whatever, and *vice versa*'. On his view, the kind of terms that can be equal are quantities, while the kind that can be greater or less are magnitudes. An actual foot-rule (i.e. a rigid 1 ft long measure) is a quantity, whereas its length (1 ft) is a magnitude. Now a quantity is capable of quantitative equality to some other quantity, and the two are *equal* if they have the *same* magnitude. Hence magnitudes are more abstract than quantities. It also follows that, whereas sameness is the opposite of difference, things that are equal are at least numerically different. A further difference between magnitude and equality is that, while the relations of greater and less (besides being transitive) are asymmetrical and irreflexive, all relations of equality (apart from their transitiveness) are symmetrical and, each within its proper field, reflexive.[5]

We pass now to Aristotle's next set of problems in this context. Instead of making ambiguity, or (as previously) the lack of a sufficient resemblance between properties, responsible for the incomparability of objects or of certain changes in objects, he advances the notion that if attributes of objects *differ in kind*, comparison between the objects becomes impossible. This discussion concerning differences of kind is not unrelated to Aristotle's previous argument about the ambiguity of words. 'Sweet' is ambiguous, because it can mean sweet water, a sweet voice or a sweet nature. And so, as we have seen, is the word 'sharp'. But instead of talking of the ambiguity of the one word 'sweet' (or 'sharp'), one can say that attributes such as sweetness (or sharpness) vary with different kinds of subject matter (such as water or voice for sweetness, and wine, pencil or tongue for sharpness). The attributes in question, then, will be *un*ambiguous, inasmuch as there is only one kind (or meaning) of sweet water, or one kind (or meaning) of sweet voice; and this applies similarly to sharpness of wine, pencil or tongue. The concept of verbal ambiguity will disappear altogether in cases where there is a difference of kind between properties, without there being one word that could be applied to all. Thus an object may be warm, sweet and white, with no one single word that could be applied to all three properties in a different sense.[6] But even if one and the same word, say 'great', is applied to properties which are different in kind, such as a volume of water and a volume of sound, one might still prefer to say that a great volume of water differs in kind from a great volume of sound rather than that the word 'great' itself is ambiguous. The same applies to the word 'equal'. Rather than say that this word itself is ambiguous, one could speak of it as applying (though in each case in a different sense) to subject matters that differ in kind. For instance, a vessel filled to the brim with a certain volume of water would be equal (in size) to another filled to the top with the same volume. But a voice producing a great volume of sound would be equal (in strength) to another producing the same volume of sound.

If attributes differ in kind, it is likewise logically impossible to compare one with the other and ask, for instance, whether a lump of sugar is sweeter than it is white, or whether a given volume of water is equal to that of a given volume of sound (though, of course, it makes perfectly good sense to ask which of two lumps of sugar is whiter or sweeter respectively, and whether a particular horse is as white as a particular dog or as small as a particular donkey).

Aristotle (rightly) denies that the difficulty of comparison in cases of differences of kind is removed by acceptance of Plato's doctrine of 'Forms': that is to say, he does not believe that there is an ideal or absolute sameness, equality, sweetness and whiteness, and that these have different 'material' applications in different subject matters or recipients.

Another way in which to express the difficulty over comparisons, as Aristotle sees it, is to point out that some qualities, such as colour, form a genus which can be logically subdivided into species with their attendant differences. In cases like these, he argues, comparisons cannot be made within the genus itself, but only within each of its species. Thus one can say that one thing is whiter than, or as blue as, another in the specific sense of colour, but one cannot say that it is more 'coloured' than another in the general sense of colour. By the same token, it would be impossible to speak of one thing as being bluer than another is green, or that it is as blue as another is green.[7] The lesson Aristotle draws from this argument is that attributes of objects are comparable with each other (in terms of being 'the same' or 'more' or 'less') only if they do not differ from one another specifically. For if they do, they form a genus, and in this capacity can be as little compared with one another as 'being coloured' can be compared with 'being coloured', or 'being white' with 'being blue'. In the light of this reasoning, the previously established impossibility of comparing a qualitative change with a change of place is that these are species of the genus 'change' and in this capacity admit of no comparisons in terms of equality or of a common measure. For the same reason, if locomotion is taken to be a genus and not a species, circular and rectilinear motion are not comparable and cannot therefore be of equal velocity or cover equal distances, seeing that line too is a genus divisible into species with specific differences. To say that locomotion can take place by different means, e.g. by walking or flying, and that these mark two distinguishable species of the motion concerned, is to confuse differences in the fashion of the movement (which do not affect the question of the comparability of speed) with specific differences.

Lastly, Aristotle considers how one should attempt to discern or determine specific differences, or differences of kind in general. This question is of vital importance for his purpose of defining the equality of things and the limits of significant comparisons between attributes. He has shown to his own satisfaction that *within* a genus no comparisons are possible across the borders of specific differences –

for otherwise it should be meaningful to ask which of two things is the more coloured in the generic sense of 'colour'. By the same token, no comparisons *between* genera themselves or across the boundary-lines of generic differences are feasible. For if they were, it would be meaningful to ask which of all the different kinds of living beings is more within, or of, the category of animate being, in the super-class sense of 'living being'. It follows that only within the same indivisible species can it be meaningful to draw comparisons and to ask questions such as 'which is the whiter?' or 'which is the sweeter?'. Hence it would be senseless not only to state that a thing is sweeter than it is white, but also (on account of the ambiguity of the word 'sweet' and its different uses in different contexts) to say that sweet water is sweeter than a sweet voice. This consideration leads Aristotle to inquire into the nature of the modifications of quality and the manner in which they can be compared with one another. He rightly wishes to disqualify the statement that a lump of sugar loses its sweetness in the same way as it loses its whiteness, or that a voice loses its sweetness more slowly than does water. The right condition for comparing changes of quality and the velocities in such changes is where the quality, the change and the velocity are all unambiguously of the same sort. Thus it is meaningful to speak of one man regaining strength rapidly after illness and another slowly, and for the two men to do so at the same time. And it is also possible to speak of equal speed in recovery, since the species of change involved is one and the same, as is the time occupied by two equally fast recoveries of health.

Aristotle concludes by asking what exactly is modified when two men recover their health equally fast. He rules that in using the term 'equal', one refers to the category of quantity, and that therefore the term cannot be employed in the present context – which falls into the category of quality.[8] However, according to him, if becoming healthy is a modification of quality, the term which corresponds to that of equality in the category of quality is likeness or sameness. And thus to talk of equal velocity is to talk of two or several bodies undergoing the same change in the same time. Aristotle's observations here are on the right lines, particularly in view of Russell's distinction between quantity and magnitude, to which I referred earlier. One would say of two quantities, e.g. two rooms, that they are equally warm or equal with respect to warmth, if the quality they have in common, i.e. the warmth, is the same or of the same degree. The rooms would then be equal in that they have the same (degree of) warmth. If health is present in two men to a like extent, i.e. neither more nor less in one than in the other, their state of health is the same; the men would then be equally healthy, or equal with respect to their health. And if two walls are whitewashed, they are equal in that they have the same colour.

Five conclusions may be drawn from Aristotle's strict definition of equality.

1. For the concept of equality to apply, there must be at least two numerically different quantities or particulars.

2. In most, if not all, cases, the quantities or particulars in question will be found to differ from each other in some additional respect(s); for instance, one foot-rule may be made of wood and another of metal, and while one is old the other may be new.

3. The respect in which certain particulars are equal would be, in Russell's terminology, a magnitude, and in Aristotle's slightly wider sense, a *quale*; for the particulars involved, the magnitude or *quale* would then be alike or even identical.

4. In order for comparisons to be valid, the terms used to describe magnitudes or qualities must not be ambiguous, as are, for example, 'quick', 'great', 'sharp' or 'sweet'.

5. For comparisons concerning the equality of quantities or particulars to be meaningful, it is also necessary that the magnitudes or qualities compared should belong to the same species. Whiteness and health cannot be compared, nor can being whitewashed and being restored to health. The same applies to comparisons of modifications of qualities with other changes such as locomotion. As a general rule, then: (a) if the subjects of change differ in kind, their changes will differ in kind; (b) if the subjects differ specifically, their changes will differ specifically; and, as Aristotle adds as an afterthought, (c) if the subjects differ individually, there may also be individual differences between their changes, no matter how alike these may be in a given relevant respect.

Much of what Aristotle has to say about the strict definition of 'equality' in the logical as well as the physical sense of the word seems to me of great interest, not only in its own right and in connection with other parts of his doctrine but also, more generally, in the social sphere and for the political philosopher of today.

(ii) A WIDER DEFINITION IN THE *METAPHYSICS*: COMMON TERMS AND CATEGORIES

In the previous section I have discussed Aristotle's strict definition of 'equality' in the *Physics*, which excludes any vague sense that may be given to the word. At the same time, a case has been made for a variety of uses of the word 'difference'. In this section, attention will be drawn to an elaboration of the concepts of both equality and difference in Aristotle's writings on logic and metaphysics. Whereas in the *Physics* he emphasised that comparisons of equality must be confined to within a given species, he now widens their scope in that he allows them to be made within any one of his ten categories (his list of ultimate types of descriptive terms or empirical concepts), though with a different meaning in each.

The points Aristotle raises in this logical context reflect the nature of some of the issues embedded in his observations on political society. The issues there were, first, the diversification of the parts and functions of the state within civil society, and secondly, the real problem of establishing a generally acceptable equality between citizens who contribute to the common good by means of different trades, occupations and public offices. Very broadly, then, the analogy to be taken up here, at least on a provisional basis, is between (a) a civil community *(koinōnia* or *to koinon)*, united by a common aim and by common action on the part of its members, who none the less differ from one another with regard to their social class, their professional occupations, their public functions, and above all their manifestations of civic excellence; and (b) common terms *(ta koina)* present throughout the whole range of significant communication (i.e. in discourse on any topic whatsoever) by virtue of their purely formal or logical nature, but undergoing changes of meaning from one compartment of knowledge to another. The following is an outline of Aristotle's views on 'common terms' or what he sometimes calls 'intelligibles'.[9]

There are many passages in the *Metaphysics*, and his other writings, where Aristotle refers to 'being' and 'unity' as 'syncategorematic' words or what are nowadays called 'logical words'. In *Metaphysics*, Γ, Chapter 2,[10] he talks of the science which deals with such words as 'generically one', and he mentions as its subject matter, in addition to the notions of being and unity, those of sameness and similarity 'and other concepts of this sort'. Further on (1004 a 17–20) he specifies some of these other concepts as plurality, negation, difference, dissimilarity, inequality, and indeed contrariety itself. Since the equal is the opposite of the unequal, it is evident that whatever Aristotle has to say about being or unity also applies to equality. In fact, equality is explicitly mentioned later in the chapter (1004 b 13), coupled towards the end with further examples of 'this sort of concept' such as completeness, prior and posterior, whole and part.[11] Elsewhere,[12] he speaks of the equal and unequal as relational terms referring to numbers and particularly to unity. He ranks them together with 'like' and 'same', explaining (as he does in the *Physics*) that things whose substance is one are the same, whose quality is one are like, and whose quantity is one are equal.

Now, just as Aristotle labels 'being' and 'unity' as 'common terms', and the principles expressing truths about being and unity as 'common principles',[13] so he treats 'equal' and 'unequal' as common terms, and the maxim that 'equals subtracted from equals leave equal remainders' as a common principle.[14] The importance he ascribes to these common notions is that all the different sciences have a share in their use[15] (and so also the different *kinds* of study or topic which the sciences represent, e.g. astronomy, geometry, medicine or politics). What applies to being, unity and equality, of course, applies to such syncategorematic terms as 'some', 'all', 'not', 'and', 'or', 'implies', 'very'; they also include 'good', as we have seen in connection with Aristotle's concept of a 'good' citizen.[16] A characteristic of all common terms is that they are peculiar to no one special scientific discipline ('topic-neutral', as Gilbert Ryle has called them),[17] but are common to (or, as Ryle puts it, 'pervade') them all.

In a similar way, J. L. Austin[18] speaks of 'the same', 'one', 'real', 'good', as *substantive-hungry* or *dimension-words*. His reason for the terminology is that the words in question do not have one single and identical meaning like 'yellow', 'horse' or 'walk', but are general in application and are in fact the most comprehensive terms. In his view, these words have a dimensional character because they can be employed within each of the many compartmentalised fields of study or interest. As Austin remarks, 'even Aristotle saw through this idea'. To my knowledge, the first to point to this, still relevant, aspect of Aristotelian doctrine was R. G. Collingwood.[19] As he expressed it, Aristotle showed that the concepts of good, unity and reality 'overlap', 'transcend' or 'diffuse' themselves 'across the divisions of the categories'.

Thus we can speak of *one* star, one group, one colour, one pleasure, one resemblance; *the* circle, the fighting, the most beautiful, the quick and the dead; a *good* doctor, good light, a good heart, a good likeness; the *existence* of God, of light-waves, of the state of Israel, of a square number between 5 and 10; and of *equal* terms, equal sides, equal ease and equal temperament. On the other hand, 'chlorophyll' is properly used only in the context of botany, 'meteor' only in connection with astronomy, 'fossil' only in geology, 'feudalism' only in history, 'asthmatic' only in medicine, 'legislative' only in politics, 'hypnotise' only in psychology, and 'capitalism' only as part of the terminology of economics.

It is not surprising that there are two lines of inquiry on Aristotle's part in connection with an interpretation of the meaning of such words as 'existence',[20] 'unity' and 'equality' (for convenience' sake I choose the expression 'EUE', to stand for these and the other logical words I have mentioned). The first consists of attempts to show what 'EUE' is not, namely a characterising or descriptive word, and that it does not therefore signify an empirical or 'material' concept (to adopt Ryle's terminology again). The second consists of attempts to show what 'EUE' is, namely a logical word, standing for a 'formal' concept.

Under the first heading, Aristotle endeavours to bring out the non-descriptive meaning of 'EUE' by dissociating it from the most fundamental concepts used in the description of reality. Thus he denies that 'EUE' is a generic word or that it occurs anywhere in the classificatory scheme of genera and species. On the contrary, he asserts that, unlike material concepts, the word applies within each genus and each progressively narrower sub-species. Next, he rejects the identification of 'EUE' with words connoting substance, for the reason that nothing which is common or universal, in the sense of being present in many things at the same time, can be a substance, which is necessarily particular or individual.[21] In the third place, Aristotle explains that 'EUE' cannot represent an element in things, since elements differ from compounds, whereas 'EUE' can be predicated of compounds as well as elements. Finally, there is evidence to show that for him, since 'EUE' is not a generic word, it cannot stand for the essence of anything, and consequently does not form part of any definition. In other words, his view is that to ask: What is the nature of a thing, is one question; but that to ask: Whether this thing is existent, or is one, or is equal to something else, is another altogether different question. Elsewhere he suggests that such phrases as 'to be', 'to be one'[22] or 'to be equal' are too incomplete to be significant of any fact; something else, i.e. certain categorematic words, must be added for them to become truly informative. The upshot of the arguments so far is that these phrases, or 'EUE' for short, (a) are not descriptive of anything that exists in the world, (b) are not used in any one particular department of knowledge as opposed to any other, and (c) can be applied in connection with every one of them (though with varying senses in each).

What then does the expression 'EUE' mean for Aristotle? His attempts under this second heading are formulated in one of his most emphatic doctrines. He insists that there are 'many senses in which things are said to be',[23] and hence many senses in which they are one, or equal to something else. In its specific formulation, the doctrine states that the several senses in which things exist (or are one, or equal) arise in connection with the ten categories of being, i.e. substance, quality, quantity, relation, space, time, activity, and the rest. Regardless of whether they are interpreted as the most general types of predicate terms or as the most basic modes of being, the Aristotelian categories are supposed to cover everything that forms part of reality: Socrates or a particular tree would fall under substance, 'soft' or 'red' under quality, 'heavy' or 'tall' under quantity, 'larger than' or 'north of' under relation, and so on. The fact that 'to be', 'to be one', or 'to be equal' can be applied in connection with concepts of different type and content shows that on Aristotle's view these expressions have no descriptive or material content of their own, and must therefore, like 'all', 'and' or 'not', represent formal concepts. The same fact shows why Aristotle thought that it is incorrect, if not futile, to search for the elements of all existing or equal things in the Platonic manner, as though things, by the mere fact that they exist (or are equal to something else) could have something qualitatively in common. Finally, it should be clear that the logical expressions I have mentioned take on a different meaning in each of the ten categories. The sense of 'exist' or of 'being equal' in relation to a substance would be different from that relating to a quality, and this in turn from that relating to a quantity.

It follows that, on Aristotelian premises, it is a mistake (a 'category' mistake) to employ predicate words connoting, for example, a quantity in relation to the mind, which is unextended, or to state that a sound that is audible is the same as a certain wavelength in the air. But just as terms falling under one category cannot be defined by those of another, so it would be erroneous to assume that, just because light-waves, the state of Israel and a square number between

5 and 10 exist, these three are existents of the same kind. A conclusion like this would involve a category confusion and a 'systematic ambiguity', because (in Ryle's words)[24] 'the senses of "exists" in which the three subjects are said to exist are different and their logical behaviours are different'. The same applies to the formal concept of equality. This, as we have seen, can occur in different kinds of context, indicated either by Aristotle's categories or by various other types of discourse, each with a unique character and with its own descriptive as well as logical form.

Aristotle is right in pointing out that 'equal', no less than 'exist', is too incomplete a formula to contain information about reality. He considers that in order to be fully descriptive, these phrases have to be employed in connection with propositions asserting matters of fact under either one or the other of the categories. If interpreted in this way, the concept of equality acquires a considerably wider meaning than that which we have encountered in Aristotle's attempt to equalise builders with shoemakers on the social plane, or in Russell's merely logical analysis of the relationship of equality between quantities. One might say, for example, that Hobbes and Locke are equally famous as philosophers, that the sounds of an oboe and a flute are equally pleasing to the ear, that two geographical places are equally suitable as sites for new airports, that John and Mary are equally in love, and that Smith and Henderson are equally active in politics. Indeed, one could cite examples of further applications of the concept, as for instance when we say that a person is equally interested in history and theology, that the actual power output from a car's engine equals 50 brake horsepower, that a rope's toughness is equal to a load of 1 cwt suspended from it, or that the boiling point of water equals 100° centigrade. We can also say that an A mark equals a percentage mark of 70. However, doubts arise about the propriety of further extending the use of the word 'equal', if this extension involves stepping across the lines of demarcation between different categories or between one context of application and another. Thus, if one boy gets a 60 per cent mark in Latin and another the same mark in mathematics, it remains uncertain whether such an assessment proves that the boys are equal in intelligence or in their power of concentration. Similarly, is it possible to speak of two equally able men, if one is a sculptor and the other an accountant? Again, can a musical sound and a colour in a painting be equally pleasing, or a person be equally interested in history and himself? Certainly, a mile and a period of waiting cannot be equally long, nor can a diamond and a pianist be equally brilliant.

What these examples show is that, like 'exist' or 'to be', the word 'equal' or the formal concept of equality differs in meaning in accordance with the nature of the context in which it is employed; that it is therefore liable to give rise to paradox if used for the purpose of establishing comparisons between different types of discourse.

Now, if one is to clarify the notion of formal, as opposed to that of material, it is not sufficient to mention only the negative feature of 'topic-neutrality'. What is called for is (a) the elucidation of the nature of the difference between various formal concepts, and (b) the provision of a positive rule in accordance with which it can be ascertained which words fall into the class of logical words, and which do not. Ryle, in the letter I have quoted, continues:[25] 'As you say, there is more to the notion of Formal than "non-proprietary"; but Plato and Aristotle (and Hume) did not extract this. Nor, I think, does, e.g., Quine or Russell. They just *list* a lot of "logical words", without bringing out what qualifies a word to get into the list.'

While the latter issue, (b), is not within my present scope, the former is of sufficient interest to encourage two further comments. When Aristotle talks of philosophy as the science which studies such concepts as sameness, equality, priority, 'and the others of this sort',[26] he also ascribes to it the inquiry into 'axioms'.[27] He maintains of axioms, just as he maintains of logical words, 'that they hold good for everything that is, and not for some special genus apart from others'. They are thus just as common as 'common notions'[28] or common terms. The fact that axioms are classified by Aristotle together with logical words reveals the heterogeneous nature of the formal in philosophy, for it is made up of propositions as well as words, truths as well as meanings. Another feature that differentiates between the members of the class of the formal is that some, though by no means all, can be used to qualify each other. Obviously 'if' cannot qualify 'the', nor can 'genus' qualify 'and'. But 'equally' can qualify not only a material concept, as in 'Charles and Mary are equally in love', but other formal concepts like 'similar' or 'near', as in 'James and Lucy have an equal resemblance to their mother', or 'my house and yours are equally near the station'. Again, 'equal' can qualify 'good', as in 'he is equally good at playing the flute and the piano', or 'he is equally good at school work and games'.[29]

There is one further point I wish to mention – Aristotle's 'deduction' of the concept of the equal from that of the one. As he explains in his *Metaphysics*, Γ, Chapter 2,[30] the science which deals with such concepts as sameness, similarity and 'the others of this sort' also investigates the listing of contraries among logical words.[31] In *Metaphysics*, I, Chapter 3, he specifies some such pairs of opposites, and declares that all are reducible to the one and its contrary – the many.[32] To the one, he asserts, belong the same, the like and the equal, and to plurality the other, the unlike and the unequal. He proceeds to enumerate several meanings of sameness, likeness and their opposites, according to his statement in Γ, Chapter 2, that, 'since there are many senses in which a thing is said to be one, these terms also will have many senses'.[33] It follows that equality and inequality, on his own showing, must each have several meanings. And since, in his view,[34] being and unity have as many meanings as there are categories, and since neither is employed within any one of the categories exclusively, the equal and the unequal should likewise have as many senses as there are categories, without answering to any one category to the exclusion of another. However, Aristotle does not make these two points more explicit, except that he often mentions equality together with likeness and sameness, drawing the same conclusions about the former as about the two latter.[35]

I conclude once more that an important part of Aristotle's teaching is that the equal and the unequal have as many senses as there are categories, and that in this respect they have to be treated like the other 'common terms' which he analyses in the *Metaphysics*. In other respects, of course, as I have intimated, the concept of the equal differs from (for example) that of the good, the one, or being, just as the fact that some of the words occurring in a dictionary are logical words does not imply that they are all alike in form, force or behaviour. The only explanation I have for Aristotle's separate and more specific treatment of the equal, as compared with that of other 'non-proprietary' or 'topic-neutral' terms, is that he tends to restrict the concept of equality to the category of quantity. One would expect this treatment as a result of his statements on the subject in the *Physics*, particularly in connection with what I have called his 'strict definition of equality'. In the *Metaphysics*,[36] as we have already seen, he also affirms that, while the equal, the like and the same all refer to unity, those things are the same whose substance is one; those are alike whose quality is one, and those are equal whose quantity is one.

However, it is doubtful whether Aristotle would wish to maintain here more than that, as he states elsewhere,[37] 'all quantity *qua* quantity is known by the one'. In other words, even though those things whose quantity is one are equal, it does not necessarily follow that only those things whose quantity is one are equal, or that all equal things are quantities known by means of a unit or the one. I have already given examples showing that the concept of equality can be applied to categories other than quantity. Aristotle himself, in the chapter devoted to quantity in his 'Dictionary',[38] distinguishes between things called quantities by virtue of their own nature, for instance a line, and properties called quantities incidentally, such as 'the musical', because the musical belongs to a quantity. Hence there can be equality, according to Aristotle, with respect to musicality, whiteness, and other qualities or relations. In the same chapter, he states that 'great' and 'small', and 'greater' and 'smaller', which are attributes of quantity, 'are names transferred to other things also', i.e. non-quantitative ones.

Finally, as is clear from what Aristotle says elsewhere,[39] terms derived from those of unity and plurality, such as otherness, dissimilarity, inequality and their contraries, will, like unity itself, have different meanings. As I have suggested before and as Aristotle himself explains succinctly,[40] difference can be of more than one sort. Things may differ numerically if they are separate or other, though not necessarily other either in species or genus. They may differ in species, if they belong to the same genus, but are differentiated from one another by certain criteria within the one genus. There is difference of kind, if the ultimate subject matter of things is so different that they cannot be analysed into one another or each into the same thing. Examples would be form and matter, or the real and the imaginary. There is the more fundamental distinction between the different categories of being, such as substance, quality, quantity, relation, space, time, and the rest.

From all this it should be possible to infer with some justification (1) that the concept of equality, in Aristotle's system of thought, can be applied (a) to things which differ numerically, and (b) also within each species; (2) that different senses of equality arise in each different context, as for instance in each different species, kind, or category; and (3) that therefore, without committing category mistakes, no comparisons of equality can be established if these cut across the boundary-lines between species, kinds or categories. Hence, though 'equality' is a common term and as such stands for a pervasive concept, it does not *per se* indicate common features or refer to what is common to all parts of a given whole – such as the state.

Having considered in depth Aristotle's views on equality both in the context of his physico-logical examination and as part of his wider inquiries into formal concepts, I propose to resume my assessment of his analysis of the principle in political terms and in relation to life in civil society.

3 Justifiable Inequality and the Different Kinds of Civic Excellence

(i) DIVERSITY AND EQUALITY IN POLITICAL SOCIETIES: THE MIDDLE CLASS

First, we must look again at Aristotle's use of the word *koinon* in the context of political life. In the opening line of the *Politics*[1] he asserts categorically that each state is an association or a 'communion' (*koinōnia*). Elsewhere,[2] he remarks that if a constitution is to survive, all members of the state must combine actively to promote its continuance. He also observes that men are drawn together in society by a natural impulse and by some common interest in the enjoyment of the good life.[3] In the *Nichomachean Ethics*,[4] he takes up the point by stressing that there are other forms of community, such as a household, a village, religious guilds, social clubs, and also the relations between buyer and seller, and he notes that in each some principle of justice as well as of friendship usually exists. These particular forms of community, he considers, are all parts of the political one. However, whereas the former aim at particular advantages or at what is temporally expedient, the aim of a body politic is for the common advantage and for the good of life as a whole.

Now, as we have seen earlier,[5] if there is common action or a commercial exchange between people, the people in question might well be different if not unequal, though they will share sufficiently in some general interest to feel impelled to undertake the common action or the mutual dealings. These two qualifications – that of being different and that of having common interests – are of equal importance in any form of association. In the case of the state, the two characteristics of difference and of forming one common entity

41

are particularly pertinent. I have already discussed some of the differences involved, and I shall have more to say on this point later. First, therefore, I shall examine the common factor as described by Aristotle in the *Politics*. In one passage,[6] he refers to the state as being (internally) active and to its different members as having many relationships and connections with each other. In another,[7] he speaks of the state as a 'compound', i.e. a whole composed of different 'parts'.[8] However, what he says elsewhere about this 'compound' indicates that this notion is far from being clear, and in fact conceals assumptions which are, *prima facie* at least, incompatible.

One aspect of the state as a compound is that in this capacity it forms 'one common entity' (*hen ti koinon*), and that its parts are made up of a ruling element and of elements subject to rule.[9] If this is the idea underlying Aristotle's notion of a political compound, it involves the concept of a hierarchy and the distinction between an élite and the mass, or at any rate between rule and subordination. In this case, his conception is more about grading and differentiation than about a communion between parts. In fact, he goes so far as to observe that 'a city, or every other systematic whole, is most properly identical with the most authoritative element in it'.[10] Here the concept of equality disappears without trace.

Aristotle's other point about the state as a compound is that in this capacity it forms 'one generic unity' (*hen ti to genos*).[11] The meaning of this phrase is that in a single whole or class there must be one thing common to all its members. This one thing is the genus, and things whose genus is one are themselves one in kind. In Aristotle's example,[12] just as horses, men and dogs are of one kind because all are members of the animal class, so citizens of a state are of one kind in that they are all members of a political community. Now, this analogy is by no means straightforward, for whereas animals do indeed form a class, 'community' is not a sort-word but a collective term. As I have explained in connection with Aristotle's strict definition of equality,[13] in the case of a genus (which can be subdivided into species) comparisons can be made not within the genus as such, but only within each of its species. Aristotle's example of a genus in the former context was colour; in the present it is the state. But whereas it is one thing to say that no object can be more coloured, in the generic sense of 'colour', than any other, and no animal be less of an animal than any other, it is an altogether different thing to say that no member of a political association can have either more or less of that which is common to all. In the former case, the statement is about a class word and a universal property and, in Aristotle's eyes if not generally, is true. In the latter case, that concerning a political association, the statement is about a collective term and a multiplicity of social functions and relationships, and in this context it is most certainly false. For, to take two examples, civic virtue may not be distributed evenly among all citizens, and the contribution to the state of one section among them may be either greater or less than that of any other part of the civic body.

Aristotle's analogy is thus weak, if not invalid. Nevertheless, there is a close and significant parallel between his views on the structure of a community on the one hand, and the logic of common terms in relation to class-words on the other. As we have seen, though 'equality' is a common term and as such stands for a pervasive concept, it does not on that account indicate common descriptive features in the different categories or fields of discourse in which it is applied, but rather varies in character and meaning from one generic context to another. In a similar way, although Aristotle regards the state as a 'community' with pervasive interests and collective functions, he is aware that these do not *per se* constitute common social characteristics in the different parts and classes of the body politic. On the contrary, his emphasis throughout, even in relation to the alleged equality between citizens, appears to rest on the different form and meaning which an equality may assume in various social spheres and in various civil communities.

But, then, as Aristotle says a little further on,[14] a state is an 'association of equals'. As Newman points out,[15] 'equals' is emphatic, so that Aristotle appears to speak of the state as an 'association of equals only'. Hence what – among other things – members of a state are assumed to have in common is precisely the fact that they are all equal to one another. The difficulty here is that the description of the state as an 'association of equals, and only of equals' is incompatible with Aristotle's own doctrine, even when he deals with the social structure required in an ideal state. For, before mentioning this crucial phrase, he remarks that the 'one thing common to all the members, and identical for them all' is shared, and that members' shares in that thing 'may be equal or unequal'.[16] The common thing he has in mind – apart from food and homeland, which are means towards a common end – is 'the best and highest life possible'.[17] He goes on to describe felicity as the highest good, and this in turn as the perfect practice of virtue. But he insists that 'in actual life this is not for all; some may share in it fully, others only partially, and some may not even share at all'.[18] He concludes that 'these *different* capacities among men will give rise to different kinds and varieties of states and to a number of different constitutions. Pursuing felicity in various ways and by various means, *different* peoples create for themselves different ways of life and different constitutions.'[19]

If this conclusion is accepted, one might still assume that some degree of equality between citizens is attainable within any social class or indeed under each of the different constitutions. However, this conjecture is not fully borne out by the available evidence. Although Aristotle describes each political state as 'one common and generic entity', he believes that the elements of difference in it dominate not only the common factor but also that of equality. Therefore his description of the state as 'an association of equals' is puzzling, even in the context of his discussion of Political Ideals (Book VII). In his considered opinion, citizens are not all equal, even *qua* citizens; nor are members of trading or religious associations. If by 'equal' he means those of the same rank or station in a community, or those with equal privileges, then again, on his own showing, the term cannot be strictly applied even in this sense. Nor would it be true to describe all citizens as contributing equally to the common end of a state, for – as I hope to show later – few do, even on Aristotle's premises. The fact is that he is convinced that 'the state is composed of unlike (or unequal) elements'[20] and also that 'it is composed of different *kinds* of elements, for similars (or equals) cannot bring it into existence'.[21]

The last quotation occurs in a context where Aristotle also discusses the idea of equality; therefore some further comments are called for. The chapter of the *Politics* with which we are concerned (Book II, Chapter 2) opens with a criticism of Plato's ideal state. In the previous chapter, he had already dissociated himself from Plato's plan in the *Republic*, according to which guardians are to share wives, children and property. Since Aristotle himself regards the state as a *koinōnia*,[22] he, too, favours the view that citizens must share *(koinōnein)*, though by no means everything. One thing they must have in common, he asserts, is their domicile: just as fellow citizens share in one state, so to have part in that state they must reside there. Now in Chapter 2, Aristotle's argument is that the kind of unity, 'the greatest possible unity', which Plato proposes to obtain in his state by means of a community of wives, children and property would produce a one-man state, and therefore lead to the destruction of the state as a collective body and as the opposite of a 'unit'. It is in this context that Aristotle remarks that the state is composed not only of a number of men but also of different kinds of men. How does he pass from this to the observation that citizens of a state are equals?

The link is three-fold: (a) a state requires diverse abilities among its members so that, by *exchanging* their different services, they can achieve a higher standard of life; (b) the well-being of every state depends on each citizen returning to others an amount *equivalent* to what he receives;[23] and (c) even among so-called free and equal citizens, who may appear identical in kind, the same principle applies: as Newman observes,[24] they each give and receive an equivalent amount of dissimilar things, not an equal amount of the same things. This serves to show that a state must be composed of unequals, for if all were either rulers or shoemakers, there would be no possibility of such an equivalence. The two facts[25] that (a) it is impossible for all to rule simultaneously, and (b) the 'natural equality' of all citizens makes it unjust, if not impossible, for the same men to be rulers always, lead to the establishment of an intrinsic difference between members of a state, even though rulers and ruled may be otherwise equal and alike. For while some citizens govern and others are governed in turn, there will be two classes of people, different in kind. Even those who form the government will differ from one another in virtue of their different offices and personal services. This again proves that different kinds of men are essential to the constitution of a state, each exchanging different but equivalent (though never equal) services in the form of different functions and activities.

A similar interpretation applies to a passage in Book IV, Chapter 11,[26] where Aristotle speaks of the spirit of a political community and asserts that 'a state aims at being, as much as possible, a society of peers and equals'. The proviso in this statement suggests that the assertion is meant to be accepted *cum grano*. Even if this were not so, the context in which the passage occurs explains what Aristotle has in mind. He refers to the middle class in a state, describing it as a mean between the rich and the poor. As such, this class represents what is good: it is free from the ambition of the rich and the envy of the poor. It will listen to reason, make for moderation, and also ensure political stability and cohesion. Hence a constitution based on this class (a constitution which Aristotle calls a 'polity') is likely to be beneficial for, and acceptable to, the majority of men. His main reason for commending the middle class, however, is that the

wealthy, because of their many advantages, are unwilling to obey
and know only how to rule; the poor, on the contrary, know only
how to obey and are ignorant of how to rule. The result is contempt
and absence of discipline among the rich, envy and lack of authority
among the poor. A state composed of only the rich and the poor,
Aristotle points out, would be a state of masters and slaves, not of
freemen.[27] Under these circumstances no friendship could exist, nor
any real *koinōnia.* In the presence of enmity, men will not even
share the same road.[28] The existence of a middle class, however,
Aristotle concludes, guarantees that men can be friends and asso-
ciates and, in this capacity, equals and peers.

This important argument shows (a) that the possibility of comparing men and finding them alike or equal is confined to the middle
class only, and does not arise in the context of the whole body
politic; (b) that, by using the phrase 'aims at being, as much as
possible, a society of peers and equals', rather than 'tends to be ...',
Aristotle is asserting that not even with time will a state develop
toward a union of men alike and equal;[29] (c) that Aristotle here
compares citizens of a state, and in particular those of a special class
within it, and not its elements or components which, as will be
remembered, he describes as unlike;[30] and (d) that, if he maintains
that political rule is rule over freemen and equals, he is thinking of
the authority of a statesman, in contrast to that of a master who rules
over slaves.[31] The contrast is analogous to that between the authority exercised by the middle class and the power wielded by the rich
over the poor.

The questions of diversity and equality in a civil community arise
in yet another context of Aristotle's *Politics.* The state, we have
seen,[32] is a compound. As such, it consists of rulers and ruled[33] and
of other necessary or essential parts, all of which are mentioned in
connection with Aristotle's critique of Plato's account.[34] Parts, as
Barker explains,[35] may denote a body of persons, or they may signify
a quality of such a body. Hence either wealth or the wealthy may be
spoken of as part of the state, the latter marking off a certain body of
people, while the former represents the property they own. Besides
possessing parts, a state depends on certain necessary conditions, in
the absence of any one of which it would not exist as a state. These
conditions must not be confused with the parts of a state, particularly not the necessary or essential ones, for the presence of all
necessary conditions is not sufficient in itself to constitute a state,
whereas the presence of all its necessary parts would be. My reasons

for introducing the issue here are (a) that some further light is cast on the factor of diversity underlying the composition of a state; (b) that Aristotle seeks, against the background of the insufficiency of the state's necessary conditions, to distinguish between proper and improper uses of the concept of equality; and (c) that in none of his writings is the notion of a true political community so extensively employed as here where he distinguishes between the necessary conditions and the operative functions of a state. All these issues are discussed in Book VII, Chapter 8 (already mentioned), and particularly in Book III, Chapter 9.

In the chapter in Book VII, Aristotle affirms that, in an ideal situation, the conditions necessary for the existence of a whole are not among its organic or integral parts.[36] After enumerating both the necessary conditions and the organic parts of a state (sects 6–9), he cites, on the one hand, farmers with their provision of food and craftsmen with their tools and skills, and, on the other, soldiers bearing arms in defence of the state, a class owning and supplying property, priests administering religious worship, and finally an assembly of people deliberating and adjudicating in the public interest. He holds that each condition and each part, together with its services, is necessary; however, he stipulates that only if all are present does a state exist and is it wholly self-sufficient.

The discussion in the passage of Book III is along different lines. Here Aristotle argues that there are indeed a number of necessary conditions for a state to exist, but that, even though all may be present, they would not be sufficient to constitute its existence. One such condition is the contiguity of places within a state. As he points out, however, if Corinth and Megara were united by a common surrounding wall, this factor by itself would not make a single city-state. Another necessary condition is intermarriage; yet again, if there were a common scheme for intermarriage between Corinth and Megara, this alone would not unite the two cities. Finally, Aristotle points to the existence of a common system of law in the state, which is intended for the prevention of wrongdoing and the furtherance of proper methods of exchange. However, he considers, even though farmers, shoemakers, carpenters and many other artisans might associate with one another for the sake of concluding commercial dealings and mutual agreements, they would still not form a state. The reason why Aristotle denies that any of these conditions (even in conjunction) is capable of constituting a state is that he postulates for its ultimate end and perfection the satisfaction of higher and more spiritual needs.[37] Full self-sufficiency, he now declares, lies in the realisation of a moral cause – the attainment of a life of superior quality – though contiguity, consanguinity and legal protection remain indispensable conditions. What he advocates is not the mere form of living together or of social coexistence *(to suzēn)*, but the achievement of a good, well-integrated life *(to eu zēn)*. Again, he equates a state not just with the bonds of friendship and other family, religious and social ties, but with the total purpose to which all these institutions of civil life are directed. Therefore the *koinōnia* he has in mind is not that of residence, intermarriage, alliance or exchange, but one where families and villages join together in a 'self-sufficient life of true felicity and goodness'.[38]

The conclusion Aristotle draws is that the criterion by which to assess the essential nature of a political association is whether it gives rise to 'good actions' and not merely to an ordinary community life. It follows (a) that those who make significant contributions to an association of this kind (i.e. by the performance of good actions) deserve more than those who contribute little; and (b) that persons of like merit should be of the same rank and have equal privileges. These two corollaries are in accordance with the principle of proportionate equality, based as this is on the relation between award and desert. The full implication of Aristotle's view, however, is that 'civic excellence' brings with it a justifiable or equitable *inequality*. For it is clear that in his opinion preferential treatment must be accorded to citizens who actively and substantially contribute to the common good as opposed to those who, in the light of the mere democratic conception of justice, are their (free-born) equals, and those who, with regard to the simple oligarchical criterion, are their (noble) superiors.

Consequently, whereas all the necessary conditions for the existence of a state are shown to have no more than an ancillary function, full citizenship, if this entails cooperation in the good life of the community, becomes an integral, supremely important, part of the idea of the state. At the same time, whilst the democratic ideal of equality and the oligarchical one of superiority pale into insignificance, the factors making for diversity in a state prevail over those constituting its common nature.

(ii) THE DIVERSITY OF CONTRIBUTIONS TO THE STATE AND THE QUESTION OF THEIR RELATIVE MERITS

Aristotle is well aware that the contributions to the well-being of a state can vary greatly, both because of the difference of potential among its citizens and also because the principle of self-sufficiency demands that the various elements should make different contributions.[39] He also observes that considerations of quality as well as of quantity are relevant to the making of every state, and he repeatedly emphasises that the qualities which contribute to its existence consist of such diverse factors as free birth, wealth, culture, nobility of descent, a sense of justice and a military spirit.[40] It should be clear then that he himself may have had doubts about an acceptable way in which the comparative relevance of all these contributing factors could be estimated; also whether, if any of the qualities mentioned belonged to one of the parts composing a state, and quantity or superiority in numbers to another, there was a reliable way in which to assess the relative merit of either part.

The issue is of considerable importance, since it concerns a question which has recurred throughout this discussion, i.e. whether it is possible to determine with certainty which part of the state is to count as equal to any other. Once an answer has been found, it would also be possible to ascertain the basis for the principle of proportionate equality as applied to *all* ranges of activity within a state. Weighing in favour of number is the 'axiom', accepted by Aristotle throughout, that the part of a state which actively desires its constitution to continue must be stronger than the part which does not. This consideration explains why it is essential for both a democracy and an oligarchy to win the support of the middle class.[41] But then, what speaks for the importance of quality is its own determining influence on civic excellence and the good life. It follows that the factors of quantity and quality must be placed in the balance against one another. This does not mean that, if quality belongs to one of the parts which compose a state, and quantity to another, superiority in quantity on the one side is sufficient to outweigh superiority in quality on the other, or vice versa. For a decision in favour of quantity would be acceptable only if the weight of the numbers involved is *more than enough* to counterbalance the higher quality of the other side. Even then, one may ask whether a democracy can be justified on these grounds alone, and similarly whether rule by the rich or other notables in an oligarchy can be vindicated on the basis of their (in this sense) superior quality alone. In the chapter under consideration, Aristotle does not explicitly ask either of these questions, nor in fact whether quantity can be compared with quality in the manner described. However, if his wider definition of equality (i.e. as applying in all such categories as quality or quantity, but *differently* in each) is taken into account, the propriety of such questions is implicit in his argument.

Elsewhere, Aristotle expressly raises questions that cast doubt on the issues mentioned. In one passage,[42] where he endeavours to improve upon accepted views on equality, he acknowledges that, though common opinion is right in distinguishing between the equal and the unequal, there is the important question that, if some people are equal and others unequal, in what way is this so? In the case of flute-players who are all equally gifted, the qualification of noble descent on the part of one would make no difference to the assessment of his artistic merit. Since better birth is of no consequence, neither, of course, is a better complexion or greater height. If this argument applies to flute-players, must it not also apply to men holding political office? Hence, in the eyes of those who engage in philosophical appraisals in politics, any argument involving an equality or a difference *in any respect whatsoever* must obviously be invalid. If excellence is to weigh significantly in connection with a given function, it must contribute significantly to the performance of that function. But nobody will play the flute better for being better-born or better-looking. If these qualities count for nothing in this context, what argument is there to prove that wealth but not noble birth, or noble birth but not beauty matters in political achievements?

The answer which suggests itself is that either wealth or noble descent, or both, have something to contribute to the purposes of a state.[43] Still this point remains to be proven, as does the contention that different qualities can be made commensurable with one another. For how can superiority of height in a person be commensurable with either wealth or noble birth, even in a context where it is relevant (such as the formation of martial habits), if it remains an open question whether an excellence relevant in one respect is comparable to an excellence relevant in another? And if comparisons between qualities involve quantitative assessments, one would have to allow that, if ⅝ of one is superior to ½ of the other, ½ of the former is equal to ½ of the latter – an unwarranted assumption. Still, in the passage under consideration, Aristotle concludes[44] that in matters political there are valid reasons for basing claims to honour and office on noble descent, free birth, wealth and military prowess – in his view all relevant in their contributions to the well-being of a state.

In another passage,[45] however, he has second thoughts. He begins by repeating that the qualities mentioned, in particular culture[46] and virtue (if one thinks of their contribution to the good life in the state, and not merely to the state's existence), have a proper claim to be recognised in the award of honours and office. He advances as evidence the observation that the rich, in owning a larger share of the land, thereby control one of the essentials of life in a state – i.e. the public economy; in addition they are, on the whole, more reliable in matters of contract. While the free-born claim recognition on the strength of their citizenship, the noble-born claim it because honourable descent is held in esteem everywhere. Besides, noble birth is generally considered a fountain of virtue. Goodness of character has a fair claim too, for justice is closely connected with other virtues, and in this capacity can become operative in social relations.[47] On the other hand, one might argue that, as opposed to the claims of individuals, the people at large are stronger, richer, and better than the few.[48] The question which Aristotle now poses is: What would happen, if these rival claimants – the wealthy, the well-born, the good, and the general body of citizens – were to fight over which of them is to govern?

Here the issue is different from the points raised previously, and it is beset with a difficulty which would seem to prove that each of the principles, in virtue of which men claim to rule, is also *improper*. For instance, if the few claim the right to govern because of their moral rectitude and regardless of the fact that they are few in number, may not a man who happens to be particularly virtuous defend his claim on the grounds of this same special quality, in spite of being the only one in this category? The claims of the few wealthy of noble descent may be challenged by the wealthiest or the best-born among them on similar grounds. Even the claims of the many may be disputed on this basis. For if their reason for being sovereign is that they are stronger than the few, one man who is more powerful than all his fellows should, in virtue of this principle alone, merit supreme command. Conversely, if the criterion is weight of numbers rather than the possession of a certain quality, the few have an advantage over one man, even though he may be wealthier or stronger than they. On the same principle, the masses should have a better claim than the few, with or without the relevant property.

Another difficulty is this. If the many, taken as a whole, are better than the few (who may be better individually), how is a law-giver to enact the right laws to the best of his power? Should he legislate for the benefit of the majority or for that of the few really good men? Aristotle's reply is that what is right should be 'equally right' in the sense that it is advantageous to the whole state and to every citizen alike.[49] The answer is surprising in view of the variety of other claims Aristotle has been arguing for. It is also vague with regard to the meaning of such phrases as 'equally right' and 'common good'. Still, Aristotle would seem to side in favour of the criterion of the superiority of the many, taken collectively. But then, a new difficulty is that, if one person were to be pre-eminently superior in goodness and political capacity, Aristotle's previous plea on behalf of such a man's supreme authority would be neutralised by his present view that such 'a god among men', who is 'a law in himself', cannot be considered part of a state.[50]

What is peculiar to this argument is not so much the implicit policy, common in ancient democratic states, of ostracising those with too much political influence. Nor is it that the argument in support of ostracism 'possesses a kind of political justice'.[51] Rather, what is significant is that such a unique man must fall outside the rules of both law and equality: he would suffer an injustice if treated as an equal, and also if one were to legislate either for or against him.[52] Besides, this one man forms a class of his own. Just as most of his qualities are unique, so must be the concept of moral goodness that applies to him.

At the end of the chapter,[53] Aristotle draws the lesson from the practice of banishing the eminent. For him, the real question is how to make best use of a man of outstanding power, wealth and goodness. Since he would not wish to recommend either exile or execution, or subjection to others, the only *proper*[54] alternative in his view is for this man to become king. Aristotle's point about the propriety of his defence of absolute monarchy is not only that this is just, since in every constitution justice is advocated on behalf of the principle of superiority. Rather, the case for monarchy rests on special grounds – those connected with the unique nature of the class of which kings are members. If this is so, Aristotle's justification for monarchy rests ultimately on a matter of logical necessity,[55] a foundation which requires no further explanation.

Aristotle advances one further argument in this context, where he considers the necessary qualifications for holders of sovereign office.[56] He maintains that certain specific qualities together with others of a more general nature are required for ensuring constitutional stability. Among the specific qualities,[57] he mentions prevention of lawlessness, especially its petty forms; distrust of devices intended to deceive the masses; a spirit of fairness such that some of the institutions of democracy can be adopted in oligarchies; a continuing sense for emergencies; careful handling of promotions or of the withdrawal of honours; and lastly, steps against private extravagance and the exploitation of office for personal profit. In connection with the general qualifications,[58] he again raises the question of their relative importance. The three qualities under consideration are (a) loyalty to the constitution, (b) a high capacity for the duties of office, and (c) a spirit of goodness and justice appropriate to the nature of the constitution.

His problem now is how to assess these general qualifications if they are not all found in one and the same person. For instance, one man may be an accomplished general, but also a scoundrel and an enemy to the constitution. Another is just and loyal, but lacks ability. How is one to choose? Aristotle suggests that one should prefer the man who possesses the *rarest* of the qualities demanded by the office. In the case of a soldier, martial skill and courage are both essential and rare qualities. In the case of the treasurer's office, one should choose a man with greater virtue than is commonly found, rather than one with the expertise demanded by the office, which is common to all contenders. Aristotle adds that, although ability and loyalty to the constitution would appear sufficient by themselves to secure the public interest, goodness of character is equally indispensable, for it serves the purpose of controlling one's emotions – which is important for the sake of the common good no less than for one's own self-interest.

Newman[59] questions whether Aristotle's criterion for the choice should not have been the man with the most *indispensable* of the three qualifications rather than the rarest. This is an apposite comment as far as it goes. However, in the *Politics*, Book VI, Chapter 8 (sects 13–15), Aristotle himself lists supreme military command and the control of finance as executive offices which are not only indispensable, but of an altogether higher order of importance. He affirms that these require wide experience and an exceptional degree of trust. It follows that on Aristotle's own principles, a good general no less than a good treasurer should possess more than the rarest of the three qualities demanded by his office.

The two problems which, in my opinion, are raised by this whole discussion are (a) how to assess the merits of offices and of the several qualifications for these offices in various types of state, if the offices, their contributions to the common good, and the types of state differ from one another in *kind*; and (b) how to apply the principle of proportionate equality to the whole compass of attainments achieved by various parts of the state, if offices differ from one another not only in kind, but also in relative *importance*.

My first problem can be subdivided into two. There is the difficulty of assessing the merits of overlapping criteria arising in one and the same office, such as ability, moral rectitude and loyalty. This issue has already been raised but not as yet settled. Aristotle explains that certain offices and the qualifications for these offices may be of a general nature, differing from other more specific ones. For instance, there are minor finance officers and a supervisor of finance; petty law-court officials and a chief magistrate; common soldiers and an army commander. The overall attainments required for higher officials are such general qualities as loyalty, courage and virtue. Because each of these is of a more comprehensive nature than any of the lesser skills to be found in the lower officials, it is difficult for them to be combined in one person. And because they represent different *kinds* of accomplishment and (one might almost say) different categories of conduct, it is difficult, if not impossible, to assess each in comparison with the others. The problem is not unlike the (at least *prima facie*) crux elsewhere in the *Politics*,[60] where Aristotle suggests that in a society with a constitutional government, i.e. a 'polity', there will be a body of people possessing military expertise, who can rule and be ruled under a system which distributes offices among the wealthy in proportion to merit. Here, it would seem, military competence, wealth and merit are regarded as having equal value for the distribution of one and the same office. Such a plurality of very general competitive standards is bound to present difficulties, and there may be no other way in which to arrive at a selection between them except through *ad hoc* decisions or some arbitrary measure. In spite of the difficulties raised by the conjunction of such equally relevant criteria, it is important to take seriously the possibility of a combination of these and other general and overlapping standards of appraisal. Similar problems arise when, for example, merit, need and efficiency represent competing criteria for the distribution of rewards.[61]

What I have said about the relative merits of a plurality of competing qualifications for a given office also applies to the question of how to assess the merits of equal-ranking offices and of their contributions to the common good. This constitutes the second difficulty under this heading. The question here is to decide which profession is comparable in status to any other, and how to assess the 'proper' remuneration for, say, a high-level administrator, a senior judge and a general. In the present day, disagreements on this issue continue, and have in fact multiplied. Among the values which have come to be questioned, those relating to wages and salaries in advanced industrial societies have proved at least as controversial as any of the others. Why should dockers be paid more than bus drivers, and in some cases even more than the average teacher? Though a Prices and Incomes Board or a Pay Policy might decide that some people are to have a 5 per cent rise, while others are given up to 10 per cent, the dilemma of justifying differentials in the incomes hierarchy remains as acute as ever. Unjust wage rates may be eliminated, but can just ones be determined reasonably and beyond dispute? And even though 'job-evaluation' may constitute an eminently practical technique, can it ever be precise, fair and consistent?

This question leads to my second problem. How can one apply the principle of proportionate equality to Aristotle's classification of offices in the state in an *ascending scale* of importance? A soldier may be of high or inferior rank. In between these extremes of military status, officers may rise from one grade to another.[62] In all stages, Aristotle considers military office as indispensable and, in the case of generals, of a higher order than any other important civic function. He goes so far as to assert that, in the ideal state, 'control of military power is control of the future destiny of a constitution'.[63] He concedes that military activity is only a means to the highest end in society, namely the enjoyment of the good life.[64] Still, this admission applies to all contributions which citizens can make to the common interest; therefore it does not detract from the supreme importance Aristotle attaches to those dedicated to military pursuits. According to the principle of proportionate equality, it should not be too difficult to ascertain the relative merits of generals, company commanders, junior officers and the ordinary rank and file. But how would such merits compare with the supreme, mediocre and ordinary efforts within groups of offices and occupations lower down in Aristotle's scale of contributions to the public interest, such as legal business, finance, religious worship, agriculture, and so on?

The question is bound to arise in connection with any of Aristotle's attempts to classify contributions to public life in an ascending order, especially where he discusses the 'necessary conditions' for a state's existence and also its 'integral parts', both in ideal[65] and in real-life constitutions.[66] Within the group of necessary conditions, it will be remembered, he distinguishes between further 'parts' or 'classes' in a corresponding order of priority, with farmers being superior to shoemakers and forming the highest class, and mechanics and day-labourers ranking lowest. Notables, in their turn, fall into 'different sorts', according to wealth, birth, merit, culture, and other qualities 'of the same order',[67] while in the constitutions in which 'the few' rule, the 'different sorts' are again assessed differently in respect of their value.

If Aristotle's principle of proportionate equality is applied only *within* any one profession or area of employment, a uniformity of ratio between award and merit for all members of that profession would be intelligible and fair. His theory should then also appeal by its coherence, though again only within the limits of any given group. On the other hand, if it is claimed that the one principle of proportionate equality applies to *various* kinds of professions within the whole of society, it has an implication which one might wish to criticise. For it would follow not only that slavery, as in Aristotle's own theory, is both natural and justified, but that (for example) a first-rate farmer with record harvests to his credit might receive less remuneration than a mediocre general for a doubtful victory in a local skirmish. The reason for this evaluation would lie in a discrimination between various occupations, and in the allotment to each of a degree of merit corresponding to the alleged value of its contribution to the good of the state.[68] The question is whether there are acceptable grounds for such differentiation, for without them the treatment involved must surely be inequitable. To place the rewards of an army officer or a civil administrator above those of a head teacher or a master builder might appear, to some at least, no less arbitrary than to lay down that red-haired people are permitted to cast twice as many votes as the black-haired.

The crux of the matter is that, whereas there is little, if any, difficulty in grading resembling members of a class, such as Pekinese, in respect of the qualities they all share, there is a major problem in the attempt to grade men in respect of their achievements in society. The same problem arises in attempts to grade artists in general (i.e. not just sculptors, painters, or musicians – which in itself would be difficult enough).[69] What makes the evaluation so problematic is that in the cases in question, the items compared do not either sufficiently or significantly resemble one another. Besides, the respects in which they would have to be evaluated are too generic, and altogether too vague, to be useful for the purpose of an assessment. In these circumstances, the apportioning of different grades of recognition in relation to different kinds of achievement must break down. The only way out of this impasse would lie in a rule to the effect that those who prove themselves best in one and the same vocation must be rewarded alike, and similarly with medium-quality and lower-grade performances in each profession respectively. Whereas this aspect of Aristotle's theory is still acceptable, his apparent endeavour to make out a case for a similar convention throughout the whole scale of social achievements is neither practicable nor theoretically defensible.

A further shortcoming of Aristotle's theory is that he has overlooked an important reason for regarding one social class, or certain of its members, as more worthy of consideration than others, i.e. need. He recognises merit, public service and competence – the latter in its two forms of natural ability and acquired efficiency. But he has nothing to say on hardship, which constitutes a sound enough reason for according a person or a whole group of people the right to preferential consideration. That this is an important right and a justifiable basis for an inequality of treatment has come to be recognised in the modern welfare state, both on general grounds and in points of detail.

(iii) JUSTICE AND THE PROBLEM OF EQUALISING THE DIFFERENT

In addition to his attempt to apply the one principle of proportionate equality to the whole of an otherwise differentiated political society, Aristotle also seeks on occasions to establish a basis for a 'common' equality between the diverse components of a body politic.

One instance occurs in his *Politics*, Book IV, Chapter 3. He begins, as in the passages already referred to, by stressing the *differences* between the 'parts' of a state. On this basis he advances two arguments, one which explains the variety of constitutions, the other justifying the variety of methods for distributing offices in one and the same state. Here we are concerned only with the latter.

The opening sections of the chapter concentrate on the types of diversity to be kept in mind for the purposes of this argument. There are first the many different families, the sum total of which is divisible into the different classes – the rich, the poor and the middle class. The division can also be into the aristocracy and the common people. The former are classified according to the small number of their members, their wealth, their noble birth or their virtue, while the common people are classified according to their overwhelming majority, their poverty or their free birth. Thence one might advance to the subdivision of the common people into various occupational categories such as farmers, agricultural labourers, traders and artisans. Besides, there is the division of the state into 'necessary conditions' and 'integral parts', and also into different, though equally essential, 'powers' such as those of judges, administrators and soldiers. All these manifold elements and functions in society form 'parts' of the state in the different senses of the word. And just as the constitutions controlled by the various parts differ from one another in *kind*, so do the parts which share in their control. It follows that in one and the same constitution, offices of state are distributed according to one or the other of the different criteria described above.

Aristotle concludes from this outline of the distribution of offices that (a) the control of a constitution may be shared by all the several parts mentioned, by a large number of them, or only by a few; and (b) the award of offices to the various sections of both the common people and the aristocracy may proceed either on the basis of the power exercised by the parts or on the basis of some common (*koinē*) equality.[70]

Newman and Barker differ in their interpretation of this passage, the text of which is by no means reliable.[71] For our purpose, however, Aristotle's thesis remains unaffected by the ambiguity. He clearly affirms that offices in a given constitution are distributed according to either the different 'powers' of the poor (in the form of their occupations as farmers, traders and mechanics, or by virtue of their numbers), or the different 'powers' of the rich (in the form of their wealth, birth and merit, or by means of some other element of superiority), *or* again according to a common equality between both classes. The difference of interpretation turns on whether Aristotle, in adding the parentheses 'that of the poor or the rich' and 'existing among both rich and poor', is referring to their power or their equality.

Since I am concentrating on Aristotle's attempts to draw up a scheme of equalisation between matters which are otherwise different, the particular issue of interpretation need not concern us. For he states unambiguously (before the occurrence of the controversial phrases) that offices can be distributed on the basis of 'some common equality'. Admittedly, without the additional phrases, this may mean 'equality common to those who share offices' and might refer either to the poor or to the rich.[72] But then, if the phrase 'common to both' refers to a power (as Newman is inclined to think), rather than an equality (as Barker suggests), the fact that the two main classes in a state are said to have certain *powers* in common shows that in this respect at any rate they can be considered equal. Such an interpretation is supported by Aristotle's assertions elsewhere.

In Book III, Chapter 6, Section 9, where he refers to persons capable of holding political office in turn, he stresses that this system of constitutional rule renders citizens 'equals and peers'.[73] He maintains this view not only because each member of the state can hold office in turn, but because the office of ruler is intended for the common good and is therefore both a duty to be undertaken by the office-holder and a source of benefit to all citizens alike. Admittedly, what he says here must again be taken *cum grano*. He regards this system as an ideal and not just as natural, for it has not survived in its original form. Besides, though citizens under such a constitution can be considered equal in that they are in turn either the rulers or the ruled, they are bound to remain different both in respect of their offices and also in relation to their abilities and interests.

In another passage,[74] already referred to in a different context, a similar point applies. On the one hand, provided there is a strong middle class making for moderation, Aristotle envisages a political community composed of 'equals and peers', who may even be friends. He goes on to say that such a state is bound to be the best constituted – its elements being either the rich, the poor and the moderately well-to-do (as Newman suggests),[75] or alternatively all citizens ranking as 'equals and peers' (as Barker is inclined to think). Whatever the correct interpretation, Aristotle's statement has to be

accepted in the light of his own three qualifications: the middle class
is generally small; the elements of a well-constituted state with a
strong middle class are 'naturally' its proper members – which indicates that they may not be so in actual fact; and thirdly, in these
circumstances a political community '*aims* at being composed, *as
far as is possible*, of equals and peers'.[76] I believe that these provisos,
together with his other reservations, make it clear that (a) Aristotle
is concerned with an *attempt* to establish a basis on which the different elements in a state may be considered equal, and (b) he recognises that such an attempt poses a *problem*.

In two further passages he advances similar arguments.

In the first,[77] he deals with the democratic conception of arithmetical equality as opposed to his own favoured principle of
proportionate equality. In connection with the latter, as I have tried
to show, there are considerable, if not insuperable, difficulties.
These arise from attempts to apply equitable rules for rewarding
merit to a political community whose 'parts' differ from one another
not only in kind but, more importantly, in the quality of their
contributions to the state. Now in a democratic constitution there
would be less differentiation and less social stratification; hence the
problem of equalising the different should diminish accordingly.
What, then, are Aristotle's findings on this issue?

He observes that the democratic type of constitution is based on
either of two forms of liberty, and that these in turn rest on different
conceptions of justice and equality. In the first case, (a), democracy
means liberty in the political sense, which consists in interchanging
the roles of the rulers and those ruled. This principle appears just
since it is grounded in an equality measured by the factor of number
rather than by that of merit. Also, on this view supreme power is
vested in the people at large, and the principle of majority-decision
in this context would be evidently just. However, as Aristotle points
out repeatedly,[78] if justice were to depend on the will of a majority
consisting of the poor, then that majority would probably take
unjust decisions and act accordingly; among other things, it might
confiscate the property of the rich who constitute the minority. In
the second case, (b), democracy stands for civil or personal liberty,
which might imply no more than 'living as you like'.[79] This, however, constitutes a merely 'negative' freedom, i.e. freedom from any
form of government interference. Democrats consider this kind of
liberty eminently suited to their general system of equality, and
consequently regard it as just. It certainly accords with the ideal of a

free life, which is the exact opposite of that of a slave who cannot live as he pleases. None the less, Aristotle has misgivings about this form of democracy too: it embodies a form of liberty which may not only be arbitrary but may become excessive, and in this case give rise to licentious living and to anarchy, both of which lead to tyranny and a total absence of justice.

Apart from these reservations, Aristotle favours much in the democratic constitution, for instance the election of the executive officers by and from all the people, the method of their appointment by lot, the stipulation that the property qualification for holding office should be minimal, and the objection to any long tenure of service. He likewise maintains that, if the most typical form of a democracy and the class of people comprising it, i.e. the agricultural one,[80] are taken into consideration, it becomes apparent that they, rather than any of the others, represent the generally recognised democratic standards of justice and arithmetical equality. But then he continues on a more cautious, almost hypothetical, note:[81] 'Equality *might* be taken to mean that the poorer class should exercise no greater authority than the rich or, in other words, that sovereignty should not be exercised by it alone, but by all the citizens equally on a numerical basis.' And he concludes: 'If that *were* the interpretation followed, the upholders of democracy *could afford* to believe that equality – and liberty – was *really* achieved by their constitution.'[82]

This statement contains two relevant points. First, in Aristotle's opinion, the democratic constitution just described is likely to embody no more than an ideal, and the achievement of an all-round system of equality must consequently remain problematic. Secondly, an equality favouring neither the poor nor the rich and vested in all citizens alike, irrespective of their class, function or contribution to the common good, is bound to conceal differences between parts of a state which, far from being negligible, should actually be stressed. The two conclusions may be summarised by stating that (a) there is more of a basic (qualitative) difference than a superficial (arithmetical) equality between the parts of a state, and (b) the differences in question are always important and generally justifiable.

In the second passage I wanted to consider, which occurs in Book VI, Chapter 3, Aristotle pursues the points already raised and asks: 'How is such arithmetical equality *actually* to be secured?' He suggests that some calculation would have to be involved in the answer, and that there should be provision for two criteria of assessment, i.e. amounts of property and personal units. Thus he starts from the idea of two equal blocks of property, each with equal sovereign power but containing a different number of persons.

The details of the calculus are as follows. There could be either one block containing 500 people each owning a large amount of property, and another containing 1000 people with small amounts, or an equal number of representatives[83] from each block who together form a single body, so that supremacy would rest with one group rather than two – an obvious advantage. The disadvantage of the property criterion (as Aristotle notes) is that if there is one person who owns more than all other property-owners combined, he will claim to be sole ruler. The inadequacy of a criterion based on superiority of numbers is that, on Aristotle's view, the masses are likely to act unjustly towards the rich. Hence both criteria involve some measure of inequality as well as some injustice. How, then, can the wealthy and the poor reach agreement over justice and equality, and also over the criteria of weight of numbers and amount of property? If it is argued that sovereignty should be attributed to the will of both classes or to that of the majority of both, such an argument would not ensure that the wills, or the majority wills, of the two classes are in agreement. Therefore a successful calculus should start from the assumption that the two classes disagree and pursue conflicting policies. In this case, a compromise solution would be to attribute sovereignty to the majority will of persons who at the same time own the largest amount of property.

For example, suppose there are ten wealthy and twenty poor people and that, when a vote is taken, six of the ten disagree with fifteen of the twenty. In such a case, four of the wealthy would agree with the majority of the poor, and five of the poor with the majority of the wealthy. Now suppose that the amount of property on each side is added up so as to determine the winning vote and the seat of sovereignty. If the joint property of the 4+15 is in excess of that of the 5+6, sovereignty would fall to that side. If the 5+6 have a larger joint amount of property, their will must prevail as law. This calculus is neat as far as it goes. But does it, on the practical side, explain how the precise numerical value of voting power according to wealth should be apportioned? Also, it is not easy to see how, on the theoretical side, the proposed system of justice could bring about any equality between people, even a proportionate equality. Again, suppose the result of the calculus is a deadlock, with the joint property on both sides equal. The only solution then, Aristotle considers, must be a decision by lot or some other similar method. This, he argues, would be an acceptable procedure, since it is also adopted when a popular assembly or a court of justice is divided upon an issue. However, whereas in the last of the three assumptions a state of equality could be established, though some additional decision procedure would also be required, in the second no argument for equality, whether numerical or proportionate, has been advanced, and the calculus is merely an inadequate expression of an inadequate form of equality.

Aristotle draws a number of significant conclusions from these examples. He affirms that *in theory* it is very difficult to establish the truth in matters of justice and equality.[84] This inference is in agreement with some of the general points I have already mentioned when raising the basic problem implicit in the principle of equality. He goes on to assert that it is even more difficult to persuade those powerful enough to gain advantage over others to abide by the principles of justice and equality. This is a *factual* conclusion, derived from the evidence that, in his words, 'the weaker are always anxious for equality and justice, while the strong pay no heed to either'.[85] Elsewhere, he makes clear that these two attitudes are connected with the partly justifiable, partly unjustifiable causes of revolutionary movements: 'inferiors become revolutionaries in order to be equals, and equals become revolutionaries in order to be superiors'.[86] Aristotle's last conclusion, drawn from the two preceding ones, is itself two-fold: matters of equality or inequality are determined either by legislative or by revolutionary methods. In the former case, the issue is theoretical, and the means of resolving it are constitutional, either directly by recourse to the law or by some other equitable procedure (such as a decision by lot). In the latter, the issue is factual, and the means of resolving it are unconstitutional, with those involved resorting to force (which may also lead to a chance decision).

These two issues, i.e. the relation between equality and law, and the changes in the status of equality or inequality resulting from revolution, require further investigation.

However, a summary of Aristotle's queries and conclusions scrutinised in this chapter should be kept in mind for what follows.

1. Civic virtue and a share in the highest good may not be distributed evenly among all citizens of a state.

2. Though equality is a common term, its meaning varies from one social context to another.

3. The middle class exercises a stabilising influence only if it is large.

4. How can the qualifications of rulers for the upholding of justice and constitutional stability be assessed?

5. What does a just financial reward or job-evaluation mean, and does it relate to natural ability, training, munificence, or merit?

6. Can men be graded in respect of their different kinds of achievement in society without any unjustifiable discrimination between the various professional occupations?

7. Both political and personal liberty can give rise to injustice, and even the democratic standards of justice and numerical equality are suspect. Nor can a purely arithmetical calculus resolve the difficulties.

Is it plausible, then, to argue that either legislative measures or the more tangible methods adopted by revolutionary movements hold out any promise of success?

4 Revolution and the Law

(i) REVOLUTIONARY JUSTICE AND ITS EFFECT ON THE STATUS OF EQUALITY AND INEQUALITY: ARGUMENTS FOR AND AGAINST

Since all claims either to equal or to preferential treatment are contestable, there are only two ways in which such claims can be finally settled. One way is to rely on formal agreements between the parties concerned, or on their tacit consent to conventions of one sort or another. In either case, there would have to be recourse to legal rules and their observance. Secondly, besides the rather latent powers of convention or the rule of law, there is the – often decisive – force of revolutionary ideas and of seditious action. This drastic way of dealing with the problem proved attractive in antiquity, and it still has considerable appeal in modern times.[1]

Aristotle specifies a variety of reasons for the outbreak of revolution. Sometimes, trifling changes are the causative factor, as when the young, resentful of those who govern, challenge the law.[2] Sometimes, a more insidious influence undermines a constitution, as when from a large class of equals or 'peers', which by its nature is a form of democracy, demagogues emerge.[3] As Aristotle explains elsewhere,[4] this hazardous condition originates with the election of magistrates on a broad franchise, but with eligibility limited to the few, such as large landowners or members of political clubs. In cases, therefore, where the body of the electorate is not identical with the persons eligible for office – and in fact consists of a larger number than that of the candidates themselves – trouble is bound to arise in the form of constitutional instability. This flaw can be present in other constitutions as well, for example in oligarchies. Newman remarks that the cause of constitutional change indicated by Aristotle here, i.e. the rivalry between holders of high offices in courting the electorate for their own aggrandisement, has been widespread in both ancient *and* modern history.[5] And just as the young, optimistic of victory, set out to challenge the law, so will demagogues, coveting office, flatter the people in a democracy into thinking themselves sovereign and even above the law.[6]

Aristotle suggests two policies for combating the hazards of dissension and lawlessness. It must be remembered, he urges,[7] that there are always those who are anxious for change and who adopt a mode of life at odds with the established constitution. Therefore, he considers, a constant watch must be kept on their activities as well as on those of the most prosperous group. The remedy for wrongs which the prosperous members of the population may cause is either (a) to appoint representatives from the working class to state offices, thereby attempting to achieve a balance or fusion between the rich and the poor; or (b) to seek to increase the strength of the middle class. The former policy consists in neutralising the advantages of one social group by giving political power to the other – a process based on an endeavour to equalise the differences. The latter sets out to achieve a similar equalisation by relying on an intermediary force which would limit the arrogance of the prosperous and the discontent of the have-nots. Either policy, Aristotle concludes, will prevent dissension arising from inequality.

Two further points should be noted in connection with Aristotle's suggestions. One concerns the nature of civil unrest and the way in which it arises from inequality, the other the possibility of creating a large and stable middle class. In the former case, Aristotle argues, there are two directly opposite ways in which the distribution of property and of political power may cause rebellion.[8] The common people tend to become mutinous if the distribution of property is unequal, whereas men of taste and refinement might revolt if the distribution of offices or honours is equal.

Turning now to the middle class and the possibility of establishing a status of equality between the two main factions, Aristotle observes[9] that in most states, especially the smaller ones, the middle class is in a minority both in respect of size and of power. Consequently, whenever either the landed class or the common people gains a definite advantage, the middle class may find itself not only outnumbered but overpowered, while the administration of public affairs might come to be vested in the hands of either an oligarchy or a democracy. At the same time, irrespective of which of these two sides emerges supreme, neither of them would be prepared to establish a constitution based on the common interest or on the principle of equality. Alternatively, if neither the masses nor the wealthy gain the upper hand in those circumstances, their disputes and struggles would continue.

The admission that disruption among citizens is more probable if the middle class is small is matched by several of Aristotle's statements elsewhere.[10] For instance, he asserts that where the middle class is large, there is least likelihood of faction, and that large states are generally more free from dissension, precisely because there is a large middle class. Furthermore, he maintains, the reason why democracies are more secure than oligarchies is due to the existence of the middle class; and he adds that a 'polity' (the middle type of constitution with a large middle class outweighing both, or at least one, of the other classes) is in most cases the best form of constitution, chiefly because it is free from faction and therefore more likely to endure. Again, he holds, the fact that the best legislators have come from the middle class is further proof of its value; similarly, a legislator should always make members of the middle class partners in any constitution which he establishes; and finally, the more the different elements in a state are blended and the more evenly they are balanced, the more stable will be their combination and the more secure the constitution as a whole. All these observations show that revolutionary change can be forestalled, minimised or overcome, if the different parts of a state are integrated, or if at least a balance is maintained between opposing parties. Most important of all, Aristotle concludes, is that the principles of the 'mean',[11] the public interest, and of equality and equity are upheld as far as possible. But then, as he is the first to admit, revolutionary change makes itself felt precisely because the exact *interpretation* of these principles is controversial.

Discussion of this essential point occurs in the opening chapter of Book V – the book covering constitutional change and the causes of revolution. Arguments advanced here bring into the open two main contentions: (a) that different interpretations of justice and equality by different parties give rise to different claims (some justifiable, others not); and (b) that conflict between these claims leads to political struggle and change. Aristotle has much to say in support of these two propositions.

He starts from the assumption – crucial for the course of his argument – that the chief reason for the existence of different constitutions is that men disagree in their interpretations of the principles of justice and equality. As he has shown previously,[12] the particular issue giving rise to difficulties inherent in all political theory and practice is not just the problem of who is to count as equal and who as unequal, but the question in what respect 'equals' *are* equal and 'unequals' unequal. And because democrats and oligarchs disagree over the precise meaning of political equality, and because they also disagree over what is meant by a fair distribution of offices and rewards, they consider resistance justified if political circumstances fall short of their expectations.

In the context of his argument that the causes of insurrection always lie in a difference of interpretation of the nature of justice and equality, Aristotle adds one further qualification. Among people who have cause for complaint, he wishes to include those who do not receive the degree of preference which he thinks they deserve. He singles out men of exceptional merit and those of noble birth. Only the former, he says, can be regarded as absolutely superior and therefore as the most justified in forcing a change – though they are the last to make any such attempt. The high-born, he holds, should also have a claim if, on the basis of their status, they consider themselves above the level of the general populace. The justification for their claim to more than an equal share lies in the common notion that nobility of descent indicates an ancestry distinguished by virtue as well as prosperity. Hence in democracies, aristocrats complain of the injustice of having only equal rights, when they have reason to expect superior treatment.[13] In oligarchies, on the other hand, the masses maintain that they are unjustly treated in being denied the privileges of the aristocracy, when they are and always have been its rightful equals.

What Aristotle is primarily concerned with in these passages is the problem of the justification of revolt. Therefore he raises the question of the legitimacy of motivation among people living under an oligarchy, who stir up sedition because they are filled with a desire for equality. This passion for equality among democrats, he argues, like that for superiority among oligarchs, 'may have some justification; though it is also true that either may be without any'.[14] Both aspects of his remark show, more clearly than before,[15] not only why it is theoretically difficult to discern where truth lies in these matters, but more importantly, why there is a practical problem[16] in persuading men to act justly – since what is involved is a man's power and self-interest no less than his rightful claim to equality and justice.

The nature of the dispute over power, equality, the common good, and the conflicting interests in community life becomes even more controversial if the issues to be interpreted assume a *systematic ambiguity*. Aristotle, no less than Wittgenstein, speaks of certain rule-determined human conventions as 'forms of life', and he particularly speaks of constitutions as 'ways or schemes of life'.[17] Now it may be true that interpretation and controversy in politics often derive their substance and direction from a plurality of perspectives, each representing a 'way of life' with its own *kinds* of question and answer in some particular context or at some particular level of discourse. If it is this which can make the interpretation of political principles difficult, clashes between disputing parties over the discovery of truth in these matters will arise not from mere disagreement but from an incompatibility of views and from talking at cross-purposes. For someone who understands a question in a normative sense (as Aristotle often appears to) must be misled if he sees issues raised as though they were founded on matters of fact. Alternatively, if a person tries to define the meaning of a concept such as justice or equality, it must be confusing to him to be told what (as a matter of sociological observation) people accept as just or equal, or about the ways in which they happen to apply these terms to certain situations in the political world. And if one of the opposing sides to a dispute endeavours to *justify* rationally and impartially the validity of a system of law and order, and another *explains* from an inside point of view the workings of a social rule or tradition, the two sets of argument will never really meet.[18] As I said, Aristotle is, on the whole, more interested in questions of meaning and definition, validity and justification. And rather than merely describing incompatible positions in the debate over certain social practices and theories, he sets out to discover what chances there are for creating a unity of political purpose in a context of diverse interests and in the face of rival claims and an unequal distribution of power. And just as he looks for possibilities of common action and reconciliation (no matter on how partial or provisional a basis), so he attempts to sort out the lawful from the unlawful and, similarly, the just from the unjust in the context of revolutionary change.

The assumption that the causes of seditious action may be both just and unjust fits in with the notion that there can be legal as well as illegal means of attaining revolutionary ends. Aristotle specifies two forms of constitutional change: (a) the constitution is radically transformed or abolished altogether; (b) the constitution as such remains intact, but certain alterations are introduced within the existing system. Here there are again several possibilities: (1) the

administration passes into the hands of the seditious party but with
the fabric remaining as it was; (2) the principles on which the
prevailing constitution is founded become either more radical or
more moderate; and (3) only part of the previous constitution is
changed, as when for example some special civil offices are created
or eliminated. Any of the partial changes described so far might be
brought about by either legal or illegal means. However, if a constitution is drastically transformed or abolished altogether, it is more
likely that the change will be produced illegally, whereas if any of
the other three (minor) alterations occur, they may be the outcome
of perfectly legal action. Though Aristotle does not draw this
distinction expressly, it is implicit in his use of the word *stasis*,
which can mean both a general uprising or social conflict, and also
opposition by a particular political faction.

Aristotle concludes that, while the cause of rebellion is always
found in a state of inequality, revolutionary tactics are unjustified
when there is no inequality, and that there will be no inequality if
men are treated in proportion to their different merits on the basis of
an equality of ratios between desert and recognition. He admits that,
though the principle of proportionate equality seems plausible to
everyone and is accepted everywhere in theory, men differ over its
application. Revolutionary action may thus arise in the light of
what people feel about this principle in practice. The result, in his
opinion, is that no constitution built on either the democratic or the
oligarchical conception will endure. The reason is that both these
constitutions are based on the initial error of interpreting equality in
too narrow a fashion. While in some cases, no doubt, the principle
of numerical equality is to be recommended, in others that of proportionate equality would represent the right course. With respect
to safety, too, Aristotle favours a democratic form of government: it
is less open to sedition than is an oligarchy, since it is exposed only
to dissension between the democratic and the oligarchical parties
and not, as in an oligarchy, to disputes within the ranks of the party
itself. A further advantage of a democracy is that it approaches,
more than an oligarchy, the most stable of all forms of government –
the 'polity', composed as this is of a strong middle class with an
equal share of power in the established government.

The remaining inquiry into the relationship between equality and
the law now follows. Since the common motive for revolution is an
overwhelming desire for equality, and since this in turn – as I
explained in the opening pages of this work – largely depends on the

idea of justice, an alternative way in which to establish a state of equality in a society is to rely on its legal institutions and their jurisdiction.

(ii) LAW AS A CONVENTION AND LAW AS NATURAL: FACTS AND NORMS

As has been stated already on a number of occasions, some of the following problems may arise whenever the concept of equality is applied in ordinary discourse: (a) the word 'equal', unless defined strictly or in the context of Aristotle's doctrine of the categories, is apt to be vague; (b) claims to equality, more often than not, are advanced when there is diversity, and particularly inferiority, among those on whose behalf such claims are made: hence the problem of equalising the different arises; and (c) revolutionary ardour indicates that practical difficulties, too, lie in the way of establishing a state of equality: the powerful or the rich become dissatisfied if their demand for privileges and other preferential treatment is not met; the weak or the poor tend to rebel if they believe that it is impossible for them to obtain equal status by ordinary means. Equality, then, in one sense at least, may be the opposite of both excellence and lack of status, and so long as either of these prevails, the prospect for equality is poor.

It is otherwise with equity and justice, both of which may at times be found compatible with excellence and with inferiority of rank no less than with diversity in general. It is possible, therefore, that when people speak of equality, they too have equity or justice in mind. It also follows that if they are presented with an alleged egalitarian position or a case of *prima facie* inequality of treatment, what they are concerned with is to discover whether the claim to equality is just or the unequal treatment equitable. Aristotle introduces this issue openly when he asks to what extent, if any, there is justice in the democrats' claim to rule on the ground of their free birth, their numerical equality or their collective strength and virtue, or whether oligarchs have a better grasp of the idea of justice when advancing their claims on the strength of some alleged superiority.[19] He also raises the question of whether one pre-eminently superior person, 'on the very same ground of justice', should be sovereign over all others, or whether, in view of his evident superiority to the rest of the community, he should fall outside the jurisdiction of the state altogether; the argument in favour of ostracism would then possess some degree of political justice too.

The issue, it is clear, is a question of 'proper principle'[20] and this, Aristotle argues, is one for legislators to decide. A law-giver 'wishes to enact right laws to the best of his power'; but 'right', according to Aristotle, is what is 'equally right'. That is, neither the interests of the democrats nor the claims of the oligarchs should be considered exclusively. However, if the proper object of legislation is to be of benefit to all, 'equally right' must mean a measure of justice and equality which takes account of Aristotle's notion of proportionate equality. For while this alone attempts (on grounds of merit) to preserve features of public life which embody differences, preferential treatment, and thus inequality, it likewise seeks (on grounds of equity) to establish a system of true equality based on ratios. A difficulty still lies in the existence of the eminently superior. Since the law in general is restricted to those who are equal in birth and capacity, the preeminent should be considered a law unto themselves, with legislation enacted neither for nor against them. Sentence of ostracism, therefore, would represent a 'sort of correction' in the interests of symmetry and proportion, and above all of the common good.

If this policy of levelling proves neither practicable nor beneficial, a legislator must frame a constitution which does not stand in need of such a remedy.[21] As we have already seen, a political association is composed of dissimilar parts, which yet are so united by common aims and common action that the rules of justice and of a proportionate equality of rewards can be made to apply to all its members. Here, the important point is that differentiation in a state leads to unity only if this is secured by principles of justice. Still, the question 'How should a law-giver proceed under given circumstances?' cannot be decided merely by turning to principles of natural justice. Rather, the answer must lie in some *ad hoc* legislative enactment or convention – though for Aristotle, not all justice is purely legal or conventional. What is true is that, in his opinion, natural justice is not sufficiently flexible to conform to all circumstances, and even when it can be said to apply, it must be left to legislators to declare in what way this is so. For just as the right hand is normally the stronger and yet men can make themselves ambidextrous,[22] so positive legal regulations are capable of supplementing the rules of natural justice, and may in fact be necessary to 'correct' them.

In fairness to Aristotle, it should be stressed that in the ancient controversy over whether laws are valid by nature or are ultimately man-made, his sympathies lay for the most part with the view that political as well as moral laws have a natural, not a purely conventional, foundation. His reasons for this position were three-fold.[23]

Political associations, like other associations, have ends or purposes.[24] In fact, to be goal-directed and to be capable of reaching the acme of a course of development, he argues, is one of the meanings to be attached to the word 'natural'. The development he envisages in the present context is not so much a physical process, or merely the consummation of the nature of other associations like the household and the village, as the formation of moral perfection within the state from an immanent impulse in human nature. By assisting men to attain their highest aspirations in contrast with their purely individual ends, political associations and their laws serve the common good and thereby prove themselves natural. Secondly, if there is an end, there is also a means to the end. This relation between means and ends is natural to the extent that it fulfils a function and creates some useful product, particularly in the case of organic developments which enable each living being to become a natural whole.

Living beings in effect secure their own growth largely by themselves, and are therefore mostly self-sufficient and, in this wider sense, natural. With the help of this analogy, Aristotle regards the state itself as a living organism with a potentiality for spontaneous, full development; hence, both morally and materially, the state may be considered self-sufficient and natural in its own right. Aristotle's third reason for drawing attention to the natural basis of a political association is that, as an organic whole, it takes natural or logical priority over both the family and the individual. This must be understood to mean that only in the context of state and society can a man become a moral person as well as a good citizen.

In the light of these arguments it might seem that, on Aristotle's premises, there would be an inconsistency in maintaining that man is by nature part of a political whole, while conceding[25] that law-givers as well as founders of cities and colonies may purposely *construct* political associations as though they were a mere artifice, and similarly *introduce* principles of justice as the result of conscious choice. However, as Barker rightly points out,[26] there is no contradiction here, for in Aristotle's opinion it is also part of human nature to strive consciously to create, frame and evolve political associations. In this sense, positive legislation no less than social education may help perfect the purposes of nature. I conclude that, although Aristotle accepts the view that both political justice and life in society are on the whole natural, he looks upon the thesis that they are conventional (put forward chiefly by the Greek 'Sophists') as complementary rather than as contrary to his own.

While a full discussion of Aristotle's belief that there is a natural law governing moral and political life will be introduced at a later stage, I must take notice here of a shortcoming in his views on this subject which is absent from his concept of positive or conventional law. He stresses that legal codes which exist as a result of human decision and may be enforced by various civil institutions are mutable, whereas laws which exist by nature and are not derived from human thought are unalterable and therefore have the same force and validity throughout. He derives the notion of an immutable natural law in this sense from the analogy of fire, which invariably burns in the same way both in Greece and in Persia, while men's ideas of justice and other legal conventions vary from place to place and from time to time.[27] The analogy cited is weak, if not altogether invalid. For the example of fire burning uniformly everywhere can be generalised into a law-like statement concerning the unchanging features of the process of combustion, which as such is a descriptive statement, whereas the dictates of an alleged natural law have a moral or legal sense, and are assumed to be prescriptive.[28] The contrast between the two types of law is ultimately that between fact and norm, science and ethics. And while natural laws in science offer no more than reliable formulations of what appears to be the invariable case, natural laws in morality authoritatively and definitely demand, even command, that men in general ought to behave in certain regular ways: in this sense, moral laws alone may be properly said to rule or govern. Similarly, if scientific laws are shown to be invalid, they can be reformulated, whereas no breach of a moral law either necessitates its reformulation or alters its validity. Again, if men's conduct conforms to a law which they accept as binding, they may be said to obey it. Stars or plants, on the other hand, cannot strictly speaking be said to 'obey' the law of their nature. 'I am bound to help my parents' and 'it is bound to rain' are two fundamentally different assertions – a fact which becomes clear once the ambiguity of the words 'obey' and 'law' is perceived. None the less, Aristotle appears to be unaware of the ambiguity, and he also falsely assumes that a moral law must be as rational in its nature as a scientific one, so that both would be revealed by a combination of reason and observation.[29]

There is more of an analogy between scientific laws in nature and positive laws in either politics or ethics in that both types of law are mutable, the former being open to reformulation, while the latter is liable to variation from one context to another. Both laws also depend, in one sense at least, on human decision. Conventional laws cease to hold if legislative bodies or politicians so decide, while the hypothetico-methodological basis of scientific laws admits of a choice between alternative systems of formulation and reference. In another sense, however, the facts on which a scientific law is based are largely, if not altogether, independent of human decision. Even then, one has to acknowledge that facts are observed and in this capacity can be *stated*, and that statements rely on formulation, interpretation, a classificatory system, rules of language, and similar flexible conventions.

Hence we must consider the factors of choice and variability inherent in Aristotle's concept of positive or conventional law, and also its bearing on the issue of equality.

(iii) EQUALITY AND CONVENTIONAL LAW

Aristotle begins with the observation[30] that procedures which are just by virtue of convention or expediency share certain characteristics with transactions involving weights and measures. The weights and measures used for wine or corn are not the same in every market: they are larger in wholesale and smaller in retail trading. In a similar way, designs or arrangements which are rendered just by human enactment are not identical everywhere, for the constitutions and other circumstances on which legal enactments rest vary from place to place. The point, then, about conventional regulations is that once they are laid down in a given place, provisions which were not considered previously now become clear and determinate.[31]

The introduction of money is further evidence of the impact of decision-making and agreement on man's conventional dealings.[32] When money became the measure of the scarcity as well as the abundance of articles of trade, it was used as a means of pricing commodities in accordance with their supply. But since, as we have seen earlier,[33] the basic standard of measurement in commerce is the usefulness of commodities, money (by general agreement) came to be accepted as the measure representative of the principle of demand. The reason why it was called 'money' *(nomisma)* lay in the belief that its existence, development and functions were all determined by either custom or law *(nomos)*, not by nature; and so it was thought to be within men's power to change its value or indeed to make it wholly useless. An additional consideration was the fact that people may not require a particular commodity immediately but may wish to purchase it later, and in respect of such future dealings money has become a means of security. However, like the goods it buys, money itself is liable to depreciation, though its purchasing power tends to fluctuate less. For this reason, 'ideally', all goods should possess a fixed price to ensure their commensurability.

The significance of this discussion of the nature of money and its purchasing power is that the economic factors mentioned could be regarded as an indication of the conventionalist character of all values, of human justice in general, and of decisions regarding equality or inequality in particular. Again, in the case of trade, the rudiments of decision-making and agreement lay in simple barter, from which commerce and retail trading evolved as institutions, together with their attendant conventions, tacit or explicit, involuntary or planned. As in Aristotle's example of the agreements between builders and shoemakers,[34] such commercial dealings presupposed the recognition of a proportionate reciprocity of action and the possibility of a proportionate equality of all goods, so that from this principle of exchange (even before the existence of money) a specific form of conventional justice could result. Mutual understanding and adjustment must have been considerable, because the times and places for markets as well as the relative exchange values for different goods remained to be fixed. But then, in this early period, certain imperishable goods (for example silver or diamonds) which have always existed came to assume the role of negotiable exchange tokens. The reason was that precious stones and metals, together with more sophisticated instruments of exchange such as a monetary currency, are 'commodity-neutral',[35] that is they could be used for the purchase of available consumer goods at all times. While the materials of exchange thus continued to be variable and even perishable, its formal aspects, not unlike those existing in linguistic dealings and the use of language generally, reached a considerable degree of stability and systematic procedure. As a consequence, further, more complex and more highly organised measures of formalisation could arise in connection with trade negotiations, methods of accounting, commercial treaties, market calculations, agreements over rights and obligations, and questions of legal administration. Some of these elements of economics in their political as well as domestic aspects are explicitly mentioned in Aristotle's discussion.[36]

Enactment and variability play their role in politics no less than in economics. In Aristotle's opinion,[37] therefore, politicians should not only consider the nature of constitutions in general, but also pay attention to the enactment of laws in relation to each constitution. He concedes that, just as one would study the ideal constitution or the best possible constitution under actual conditions, so one should learn to distinguish laws which are best in an absolute sense from those which are appropriate to a particular constitution. As he points out, however, in practice there are different laws for different constitutions. The reason is that each constitution is concerned in various ways with the organisation and distribution of offices in the state, the assignment of the seat of supreme power, and the definition of the final objectives of life in civil society. Likewise, the function of laws is to direct magistrates in the exercise of their particular office and to help them in the control and punishment of the various kinds of offender. The student of politics, therefore, particularly the law-maker, must bear in mind the varieties of each constitution, for the laws to be enacted will have to conform to the nature and needs of any given type of political association. In view of the fact that there are several forms of both democracy and oligarchy, Aristotle's concluding remark in this context is that to have the same laws in each of these various constitutions would not be equally beneficial to all. The observation highlights the character of all civil or positive law as conventional and utilitarian, that is, as a mere device and matter of expediency.

One way in which to look upon law, even in a monarchy, is to view it as the principle according to which justice lies in a rotation of office or, in other words, in the interchange of ruling and of being ruled. The type of monarchy Aristotle has in mind[38] is a constitutional or limited kingship, of which he approves, not a kingship acting at its own discretion, of which he disapproves. Those who object to an absolute monarchy, he argues sympathetically, contend that complete sovereignty of one man over all other members of a state is not only inexpedient, but unnatural and evil. For if one starts from the assumption that a state is composed of equals, then those equals must have the same rights and the same rank throughout, just as they would have a right to equal shares of food or clothing. For this reason it is as natural and just in terms of equality for each man to assume command as it is for him to submit to it. In fact, as Aristotle asserts elsewhere,[39] 'the natural system' (i.e. that of absolute justice) was followed in earlier times when men believed they *ought* to rule in turn. The remark is of interest, since it illustrates Aristotle's belief that (a) positive legislation supports both the purposes of nature and men's natural drives,[40] and (b) the existence of a law is often upheld by some time-honoured tradition.[41] His conclusion is that the 'arrangement' according to which the rotation of office is regulated is precisely what is meant by equality and justice; that order, particularly this form of order, *is* law.[42] He adds, however, that, although it might be better that the law rather than one single man – an absolute monarch – should rule, personal rule by *several* citizens is preferable to the impersonal rule of law. The several ministers of the law should then become its guardians as well as its servants, for otherwise the law itself would have no force. It follows that if it is a question of whether a single person or a plurality of citizens should govern, Aristotle's considered opinion is that, since all are equals and peers, supreme power should, in all justice, be vested in a number of men rather than in one person alone. The same point is made in the *Nicomachean Ethics*,[43] where Aristotle reminds his reader that 'the reason why we do not allow one man to rule, but law and rational principle, is that this man behaves in his own interests and thus becomes a tyrant, whereas a magistrate is the guardian of justice and therefore also of equality'.

If this is the way in which, according to Aristotle, both law and the claim to equality rule over a constitutional monarchy, the same principle must apply to an even greater extent in a democracy. However, here again it is necessary to bear in mind his distinction between various types of democracy. For in the best and most typical form, i.e. the agricultural one, the status of law and equality is different from what it is in the worst and most extreme form, in which mechanics, shopkeepers, and day-labourers dominate.

A characteristic of the first variety is that 'it follows the principle of equality closest'.[44] The meaning of this phrase is that (a) *the law determines* what one is to understand by equality, and (b) what the *law declares* is that 'the poor are to count no more than the rich'.[45] A further advantage of agricultural democracy is its balance.[46] This lies in the fact that each citizen enjoys the three rights of electing magistrates, calling them to account, and sitting in the law courts. But then also candidates for the most important public offices are elected with their appointments dependent either on a property qualification or on ability. A state governed in this way and by men of responsibility is likely to be well governed: the chances of misconduct are minimised in that the requirement of accountability and the right of consent and censure on the part of each citizen are a guarantee that those in office govern justly. Another check on the trustworthiness of the public administration lies in the provision of *laws* which ensure the creation and survival of a farming populace and with it of the agrarian and hence the best form of democracy. The function of these laws would also be to keep the property qualification (which is the basis of political rights in this type of constitution) low and at the same time to forbid an excess of land ownership together with the sale or mortgaging of an inherited estate.

Conditions are very different in the 'extreme' form of democracy, which lacks any system of balance and may not even survive unless buttressed by *laws* or customs.[47] One of the characteristics of this least satisfactory type is (as we have seen) the policy of conniving at the practice of 'living as you like'. When that happens, the people, or at least popular decrees, are ultimately sovereign;[48] and consequently demagogues, absent from states where laws are sovereign, can rise to power. This explains why Aristotle does not see much difference between tyrannical government and this extreme form of democracy: in the former, the decrees of despots prevail; in the latter, those of an autocratic populace. And while flatterers are always present under a tyranny, popular leaders abound where the multitude is sovereign. Aristotle concludes that this particular kind of democracy is not a true constitution, not even a democracy in any real sense of the word. His reason is that in theory there can be no constitution where the laws are not sovereign. The basis for this remark, as we shall see at greater length later, is that a proper constitution is founded on rules which are truly general, and this requirement can never be fulfilled by the purely contingent, often even arbitrary, character of popular decrees. An additional ground is that, in his view,[49] a state should concern itself with securing a system of 'good laws well obeyed'. The opposite would be a state where the law is a mere covenant – that is, a guarantee that men have *rights against* one another. This, for Aristotle, is too individualistic a view of the functions and purposes of a state, especially if by 'right' is meant no more than the gratification of the impulse of self-interest. But such precisely is the libertine outlook in a democracy consisting of mechanics, shopkeepers and day-labourers, with rights accorded indiscriminately to all and sundry.

Even so, Aristotle is not without advice in the context of this 'worst' form of democracy, which he addresses to the legislators and would-be founders of this particular type of government.[50] His main point is that more important than the making of a constitution is its maintenance, and that therefore attention must be paid to the causes of its destruction no less than to those of its preservation.[51] The prime requisite for the safety of a constitution is the provision of *laws* (customary or unwritten as well as enacted); in comparison with that objective it is relatively unimportant whether a democracy becomes more democratic or an oligarchy more oligarchical. One's purpose therefore should be not so much to change an extreme democracy into the best form of democracy as to contribute to the survival of whatever 'right' constitution is in being. The most appropriate means to this end would be (a) to pass a law which prevents the use of the popular courts for the transfer of private property into the hands of the people; (b) to make sure that public prosecutions take place as rarely as possible; and (c) to punish severely any prosecutor who brings an action at random. Above all, arrangements must be made to ensure that every citizen feels bound to the constitution and does not regard the government under which he lives as his enemy.

The greatest vigilance, however, is required in *defence* of the *law*. As we have seen, Aristotle is aware that in all constitutions, particularly in aristocracies, trifling occasions may be the cause of insurrection, and that the younger generation – which is in any case prone to despise those in charge of public affairs – often presses for the abolition of an established law.[52] From this two-fold recognition, he concludes[53] that (a) particularly in mixed constitutions, precautionary measures should be taken against all lawlessness, especially its petty forms, and (b) every endeavour should be made by legislation to guard against conflict, particularly among the notables. The sum of his observations is that all constitutions are liable to be undermined either from *within* or from *without* – a thought subsequently elaborated by John Locke in his *Second Treatise of Government*.[54] In Aristotle's view, then, if stability is to be secured by law and by means of a more equal distribution of property and rewards, a good general rule would be for democracies to spare the rich, and for oligarchies to help the poor.[55]

In this connection, Aristotle again shows his partiality for the middle class as an equitable arbiter guaranteeing any evenly balanced constitution.[56] His chief emphasis, however, is on the status of the legislator as well as on the advantages to be derived from legislative wisdom and legal enactment. From these presuppositions he infers that a legislator should always try to ensure that members of the middle class will participate in the constitution he establishes. If his laws are oligarchical, he should aim at including the middle class in their benefits; if democratic, he should enlist its support in their functioning. The reason for either policy is that, if a law-giver has this section of society behind him, his constitution is more likely to promote the common interest as well as the principle of equality.[57] Further evidence of the value of the middle class for legislators is that most, if not the best, of their kind have themselves come from this class, for example Solon, Lycurgus and Charondas.[58] This observation, based as it is on fact, gains in importance if seen as part of a consistent argument. For what, in my view, Aristotle seeks to establish is that some of the main devices for securing an equal treatment of men, short of those dictated by revolutionary methods, must be legislative measures. If these are introduced and formulated by men belonging to the middle class which (more than any other social group) represents stability, compromise, fairness and tolerance, then an equal treatment of all members of society stands a fair chance of being accomplished.

This reasoning is reinforced by Aristotle's remarks on the significance of moral training and habit-formation for the development of a citizen's sense of law-abidance and for a just application of the principle of equality.

He raises the latter point in a chapter[59] in which he discusses some of the determining factors which go towards achieving equality. There is above all the question of how to 'regulate'[60] property, for this is one of the main issues underlying civil discord. In Aristotle's opinion, legislators who wish to enact the regulation of property and, indeed, its equal distribution among citizens should bear in mind two important considerations. First, any regulation of property ought to be accompanied by a similar regulation concerning the number of children in a given family.[61] For if this exceeds the number that the allotted property will support (even if the amount is based on an equal distribution), then either the law establishing the regulation of property must be repealed, or many people will be reduced to penury and become potential revolutionaries. The second point is that state regulation in favour of an equal distribution of property might prove defective in that, if the amount possessed by each individual is unduly large, the owners would be able to live in luxury, whereas if it is unduly small, they could find themselves reduced to a state of poverty.[62] It is evident, therefore, that the establishment of the general principle of the equality of property by itself if not enough: it is also necessary to devise a system fixing a precise and proper average amount. There is a third difficulty. Even if property could be so regulated as to allocate the same moderate and sufficient quantity to each citizen, the real requirement is to equalise people's desires rather than their property. As Aristotle later explains,[63] 'the wickedness of mankind is insatiable': once two obols were a sufficient allowance, but now that this has become a customary income, men continually want more until there is no limit to their expectations. It is in the nature of a desire to be infinite; and most people live for the satisfaction of their desires.

In view of all these three facts, Aristotle argues, it is useless to attempt an equal distribution of property. Rather, what is required is a method of *training* which succeeds in making those of a good disposition unwilling, and those of a weaker disposition unable, to indulge their greed. Emphasis therefore must lie on moral education which will ensure that a man eventually adopts a correct attitude to property. The necessary training has to be prescribed by law, though Aristotle's point is that the law by itself cannot set limits to desires. To expect this would be to expect the impossible. For laws can curb desires only if they are able to compel a person to do what he is incapable of achieving without duress, and no law, no obligation, can do this. Hence Aristotle's advice is that people's desires should be equalised – a task to be accomplished only if men are trained in this direction by the influence of the law.[64] The training which citizens are to receive need not be the same for all. In fact, a similar or identical education for everyone might produce a disposition to covet wealth or honours. Therefore the function of the law is to lay down sound and balanced principles of character-formation, in the light of which it should be the function of educational practice to *accustom* various kinds of people, each in different ways, to refrain from greed and thereby arrive at an equalisation of desires.[65]

Attention should now be drawn to Aristotle's views on the significance of moral training and habit-formation for the development of a citizen's sense of law-abidance.[66] His first point is that a constitution tends to be preserved by the observance of all its legal rules, particularly those which make for stability. He adds the important proviso (which I have already mentioned in another context) that the number of citizens who wish a constitution to continue should be greater than the number of those who do not. His third stipulation is that no form of government should allow itself to be forced still further in the direction to which it already leans. This is to say, a constitution must steer between the two extreme types of either democracy or oligarchy. The value of this principle of moderation is, first, that it is in accordance with Aristotle's doctrine of the mean and, secondly, that (if adopted) it will tend to guarantee the loyalty of the majority of citizens to the established constitution, thereby fulfilling Aristotle's second demand. He concludes by remarking that it is the duty of legislators as well as of statesmen to know which features preserve and which destroy a democracy or an oligarchy. Since these two constitutions cannot continue in existence without including the rich and the poor alike, it would be destructive for either to introduce a system of equal ownership which must inevitably lead to the abolition of both wealth and poverty.

In addition to his advice to law-givers to avoid radical measures of legislation, Aristotle advocates the education of citizens in the spirit of their own political constitution as the most important means of preserving a state. He argues that, if the young are not brought up in the leading principles of their constitution by the influence of teaching and the force of habit, then the best of laws (even if approved by a general consensus) will be of no avail.[67] The training he has in mind is moral as well as political. His reasons for this are, first, that constitutions are 'ways of life', and in this sense are of considerable concern to every individual, particularly to his conceptions of liberty, equality and justice. Secondly, men as citizens are supposed to do good and, just as any other activity requires previous discipline, so does the practice of personal virtue. On the other hand, a citizen does not belong to himself but to the state, and in this capacity his ends are common to all citizens. His training for these ends, therefore, should likewise be common, that is political in nature.[68]

I conclude from my discussion of Aristotle's arguments that he looks upon conventional law as a set of purely *ad hoc* procedures on the part of government for the furtherance of a state of equality between men. What is true of the conventional origins of equality, however, is in part also true of the origins of the inequality between men. As Rousseau put it:[69] 'I conceive that there are two kinds of inequality among the human species; one, which I call natural or physical, because it is established by nature . . . and another, which may be called moral or political inequality, because it depends on a kind of convention, and is established, or at least authorised, by the consent of men.' Elsewhere, Rousseau expresses himself differently and more in line with Aristotle's attitude.[70] He points out that there is 'a fact on which the whole social system *should* rest: i.e. that . . . the fundamental compact substitutes, for such physical inequality as nature may have set up between men, an equality that is *moral* and legitimate, and that men, who may be unequal in strength or intelligence, *become every one equal by convention* and legal right'. His only proviso, again a truly Aristotelian one, is that the conduct of governments themselves should be good, which in part means that their laws should be well-enacted.

(iv) THE IDEA OF A NATURAL LAW

Turning now to Aristotle's concept of justice as natural we should reconsider the distinction between nature and convention, between law as universally binding and law as mutable. Aristotle's own phrase when dealing with the features of a universal, natural law is 'natural justice'; however, he also uses the expression 'law of nature', and not only tends to consider 'just' to mean 'in accordance with the law', but regards natural justice as itself grounded in natural law.[71]

One of my reasons for inquiring into Aristotle's concept of a universal natural law is that this is more than the correlate of his notion of law as mutable and conventional. The two are really separate varieties of law, relating to different orders of discourse, such as higher and lower. The legislator and the judge represent two correspondingly different stations,[72] and the distinction between moral wrongdoing and legal guilt can be drawn along similar lines.[73] Again, a social practice,[74] in its general sense, such as keeping promises, differs significantly from any particular act of promise-keeping. It follows that justifying the former and justifying the latter are importantly different procedures, each involving distinct sets of rules, and each with its own logical criteria. One further, apposite illustration of how different levels of discourse can be applied to a discussion of the concept of law is the distinction between judicial and non-judicial justice. The issue here is to determine whether, on the one hand, there is justice – which may mean impartiality – in the *application* of a given law and, on the other, whether any constitutional law can be assessed as being itself just.[75]

Aristotle, who is aware of some of these distinctions, expresses them in a variety of ways. For instance, in one passage,[76] he insists that there is a difference between two senses of the rule of law – one which means obedience to such laws as have been enacted (i.e. conventional legal rules, which may not necessarily represent good laws), and another which means that the laws obeyed have been *well* enacted (i.e. according to standards of moral goodness and in the light of an impartial higher law – the precepts of a law of nature). Of course, there are difficulties in the notion of a system of axiomatic laws which, it is alleged, make possible the justification of lower laws without requiring justification on their own behalf. Aristotle, as I shall show later, attempts to overcome some of the difficulties by claiming that there are a number of criteria for the validity of a higher universal law, and that these can be defined largely by argument.

In the passage quoted, Aristotle proceeds to distinguish two further aspects of the rule of law. He explains that laws may be valid because they are the best conceivable for those obeying them. On the other hand, laws may be valid because they are the best in an absolute sense, irrespective of who obeys them. This new distinction admits of two answers to the question, 'What rules of law ought men to have?' The one specifies certain particular groups of men, or certain particular occasions for the observance of a legal rule, or certain particular reasons for obeying it. The other is addressed to men in general, to all conceivable varieties of occasion, and to an ultimate reason for the observance of all laws. In a similar vein, as I indicated earlier, Aristotle exhorts students of politics to 'learn to distinguish laws which are absolutely best from those which are appropriate to each constitution'.[77] The two varieties of law he has in mind are laws which suit certain types of constitution, or which are enacted as part of a given constitution, and laws which are separate from, and indeed above, any particular constitution.

There are a number of characteristic features in Aristotle's concept of a universal law of nature as a higher-order form of justice.

One feature is that, unlike civil or conventional law, natural law is independent of any positive legal system in relation to which answers to problems concerning everyday justice are formulated. Though the concept of natural justice has always been regarded by its defenders as applying to the moral life of nations as well as to that of individuals, to social activities as well as to matters of personal conscience, its model is not to be found in any human judicial proceeding or institution as such. In this capacity, it is more of the nature of a comprehensive social *ideal*, and must not be confused with the justice or virtue inherent in certain general social 'practices', in John Rawls' sense of the word.[78]

If it is a characteristic of natural law to be independent of civil institutions and to be a higher-order expression of justice, can a concept like that of equality (for example) ever form part and parcel of natural-law theory? One of the contentions in my own interpretation of Aristotle's doctrine is that, short of revolutionary measures, decisions on the part of legislators and administrators of the law determine in what sense men are to be treated equally or on what grounds any inequality of treatment is justified. It might follow that, if issues concerning equality were to be raised to the level of precepts embodied in a universal law of nature, they would become too indeterminate to remain part of legislative practice. And yet, Aristotle, no less than other natural-law theorists, has suggested ways in which the notion of a lawful equality and a justifiable inequality can be provided with a basic definition, if only in outline. In Aristotle's case, the relevant arguments are derived from the characteristic features of his concept of natural law itself. They are (a) that the law in question and with it the concept of equality are (*prima facie* at least) general, i.e. applicable to all men, and certainly to all citizens of a state; (b) that both concepts stand for explicit rational and moral principles; (c) that they presuppose rules of impartiality and equity as infallible as mathematical norms; and (d) that the development of a citizen's true sense of justness, law-abidance and equality relies on standards of moral training and habit-formation and on immutable traditions of civic virtue and legal practice.

What is by and large absent from Aristotle's views is any attempt to show precisely how men arrive at the knowledge of the law of nature. The usual method in connection with the subsequent evolution of this concept has been to refer to a conjunction of sense-perception and demonstration as corroborating evidence for both

the existence and the validity of such a law. In his exposition of the
notion, Aristotle neither mentions sense-experience (although he
opens his *Politics* with a reference to it)[79] nor does he invariably
refer to explicit argument. Thus one of the reasons why in traditional theories the law of nature was termed 'natural' is not fully represented in his views on the matter: he does not, like Locke or Hooker,
insist that knowledge of this law is acquired by man's natural faculties (i.e. sensation and reason), nor does he refer to the joint exercise
of these two faculties as what later theorists were to call the 'Light of
Nature'. Again, he was hardly in a position to hold that this is a law
originating from God in a natural way, whereas the positive divine
law is laid down by revelation. Nevertheless, it is true that in one
passage he does couple the words 'God' and 'reason' in an attempt
to define the foundation of the rule of law.[80]

More importantly, some of the traditional reasons for calling
natural law 'natural' are anticipated by Aristotle. There is his argument that this law is in conformity with the natural constitution of
the universe, particularly that of human beings. He illustrates this
by affirming that 'the special function of man is the active exercise
of the mind's faculties in accordance with rational principle'; that
there is likewise a special sort of work which each inanimate object,
each plant and each animal is designed to perform.[81] Aristotle asso-
ciates the human function referred to in this argument with the
search for first principles, and he suggests that these are revealed
partly by induction, partly by perception, and partly also by a
process of habituation.[82] It is significant that in the first of his *Essays
on the Law of Nature*,[83] Locke quotes these statements from
Aristotle in defence of his own arguments about the existence and
the essential features of a natural law. In my opinion, this fact
provides firm evidence that Aristotle's doctrine, in addition to his
analysis of the concept of conventional law, contains part of an
authoritative formulation and one of the original sources of natural-
law theory.

Another argument (which I have already referred to) is that the
precepts of the law of nature are the same for all men and that, like
the laws governing natural phenomena, but unlike those in different
political states, they do not vary from one place to another or from
one period in time to another. Locke's comment is again apposite.
Towards the end of the above passage in his *First Essay*, he quotes
in Greek part of the relevant opening sentence from the *Nicomachean Ethics*, Book V, Chapter 7, where Aristotle asserts that: 'A

natural rule of justice is one which has the same force or validity everywhere.' Locke then comments: 'Hence it is rightly concluded that there is a law of nature, since there is a law which obtains everywhere.' Locke may have drawn this conclusion himself or considered it (if not Aristotle's own) part of an Aristotelian scholastic tradition. However, there can be little doubt that in this argument he credits Aristotle (at least implicitly) with a doctrine of the existence and validity of a *natural* law.

Then there is Bishop Butler's terminology, according to which the only distinct meaning of 'natural' is – stated, fixed or settled.[84] Aristotle would, I think, accept that the law as natural and rational must be fixed and immutable, though not perhaps, as Butler assumed, in the sense of being fixed or settled by an intelligent supernatural agent. On the other hand, as I shall show in more detail in its proper place, Aristotle is in favour (at least in certain circumstances) of customary or conventional laws being modified in the light of social progress, and he would consider any such alteration equally natural and rational. However, when he speaks of the validity of law and bases this on a morality going back to a distant past, he is thinking of laws which (for him) have been truly 'settled' by nature. In fact, quoting from Sophocles, he refers to Antigone's declaration that the 'naturally just' is in force not only now or yesterday but eternally, and he insists that the principles of equity no less than all unwritten law, particularly the universal law which is grounded in nature, are constant and unchangeable.[85]

A final argument, which should be discussed at some length, is based on the alleged synonymity of the words 'natural' and 'innate', and on the belief that conscience is an inborn faculty issuing in a *dictamen rationis* and the knowledge of good and evil – the cornerstone of natural law. Views of this kind were widespread among moral philosophers and theologians during the seventeenth century, in the wake of pronouncements by authoritative Scholastics like St Thomas Aquinas.[86] Even here, Aristotle's contribution to this tradition, if only indirectly,[87] cannot be in dispute. He advances two arguments to prove that some basic human inclinations are natural in the sense of inborn and moral in their tendency. Admittedly, when he argues that men become virtuous by (a) their innate endowment, (b) the habits they form, and (c) the rational principle within them, he regards the impulses implanted by nature as morally neutral, unless they are directed by moral training and reason. For, he seems to believe, if nature and instinct are left to themselves, they are neither rational nor moral but purely appetitive and emotive.[88] On the other hand, when he discusses self-love as an inborn universal feeling, he accepts it, at least on a higher plane, as a moralising element in human conduct. He admits that if a man's regard for himself is excessive, it will give rise to indulgence and, like other irrational behaviour, be open to censure. However, if a person's self-regard is moderate, it will generate kindness, liberality and friendship, and hence goodness. It follows that a good man *ought* to have a reasonable degree of self-love since his feelings towards himself become the standard for his feelings towards others.[89]

In the second place, Aristotle firmly accepts the view that, although habit-formation and teaching contribute to a man's moral character, and indeed to virtue in the strict sense, there is such a thing as natural virtue. His assumption is that every man, from the moment of birth, has a natural tendency to be good, or (to put it in less empirical or psychological terms) has an inherent tendency to be good.[90] In one passage, he intimates that the moral qualities implanted by nature are the result of 'some divine causes' and are present to a greater or lesser extent 'in those who are truly fortunate'.[91] He stresses, however, that habituation and the application of rational principle – the 'right rule' – and above all long-established laws which *fix* the education of the young are required for the acquisition of practical wisdom and virtue in the strict sense. The law of the land, of course, would always represent an *external* rule of right reason to which virtuous conduct should *conform*. The truly rational principle of action on the other hand, Aristotle believes, is an *inward* principle. Therefore virtue in its strict definition must *involve* reason in the sense that a person with practical wisdom would be conscious of the right rule *within* himself.[92]

To sum up this part of the discussion: Aristotle, like Aquinas after him, believed in the existence of natural virtues which incline men to act in accordance with right reason. By 'natural' he meant – among other things – the instinctive impulses which serve the development of man's moral perfection. Reason, in Aristotle's view, can discern what is morally good for any man by an appraisal of such naturally implanted inclinations. A doctrine of natural law could readily develop from acceptance of these two premises.

St Thomas' concepts of conscience and *synderesis* should become intelligible on this basis. *Synderesis*, according to him, indicates an innate disposition to grasp 'the precepts of natural law'; conscience, on the other hand, signifies the application of these precepts to particular acts.[93] In the second place, Aquinas argues, the basic natural tendency in men is their self-preservation, which accordingly he raises to the status of the first law of nature, and in this belief both Hobbes and Locke followed him.[94] Locke, in fact, asserted that such inclinations as the desire for self-preservation and happiness ('inclinations of the appetite to good', as he called them, following St Thomas) were truly inborn. He upheld this view in spite of his otherwise wholly empiricist contention that there were no practical principles innate in the mind.[95] Finally, one moral dictate recognised almost generally as part of the tradition of natural-law doctrine and listed as the fourth law in Hobbes's *Leviathan*, Chapter 15, was that gratitude ought to be shown to benefactors. Aristotle anticipated this demand of reason, fairness and natural impulse by acknowledging it as one of the unwritten rules of justice.[96]

(v) THE GENERALITY OF LAW AND THE CONCEPT OF EQUITY

My subsequent inquiry into Aristotle's concept of law will be concerned with the nature of the various criteria he advances for the *validity* of law. That is to say, the point at issue will be the source of authority from which (according to him) any legal rule or any moral practice is derived. Although the distinction between natural and conventional law will not disappear from my account altogether, in the main it will give way to certain significant distinctions *within* Aristotle's theory of law as a basic standard for all existing legal rules and moral customs. The principle behind these distinctions is the exact opposite of the method embodied in William of Ockham's 'Razor'. Ockham's device, also called the principle of 'parsimony' or 'homogeneity', has been influential throughout the development of modern thought because of its contribution towards the unification and simplification of hypotheses. It stipulates that the number of principles of explanation in philosophy and science must not be unnecessarily increased: 'entia praeter necessitatem non sunt multiplicanda'; or that one should not make use of more than what could be achieved with less: 'frustra fit per plura quod potest fieri per pauciora'.

Now, the opposite of 'Ockham's Razor', which may be called the method of 'specification', was applied by Aristotle, after Plato had already sponsored it and before it was advocated by Kant, Schopenhauer and modern philosophers such as Ryle and Wittgenstein. The Aristotelian approach demands that the number of different principles of explanation should not be unnecessarily limited. Kant's formulation of the method is sufficiently relevant to be quoted: 'It is of the utmost importance to *keep apart* forms of knowledge or truths which are distinguishable from others in kind and origin and carefully guard against confusing them with others with which in ordinary usage they are frequently combined.'[97] It is probably true that 'Ockham's Razor' has been mentioned and applied more often than the method of specification. One reason for this may be that, on the whole, we notice comprehensive syntheses between things more readily than we do subtle differences. Nonetheless, throughout the history of thought, one of the main concerns of philosophers has been to draw hard and fast lines of demarcation between different categories of thought or between different types of discourse. Schopenhauer was convinced that the rigorous employment of this method would lead to great advances in philosophy, especially in connection with his own analysis of the principle of sufficient reason. For this enabled him to differentiate sharply between four fundamental ways, the 'Fourfold Root', of explaining reality, i.e. in terms of being, becoming, knowing and acting. The principle also achieved for him a clear distinction between the idea of logical necessitation on the one hand and that of causal necessity on the other.

A similar variety of explanations can be advanced in answer to the question, 'What is the nature of law and of its binding force?' The question is open to several answers because it admits of a number of different senses. One might ask, 'What is the necessary condition for the existence of a law?' or, 'What grounds are there for speaking of something as a law?' Neither of these questions is identical with the problem 'On what grounds people do, or ought to, obey a law?' Aristotle's questions concerning the law, and his replies, are equally varied. Indeed, it is important to point out that his achievement, in this as in other contexts of philosophical importance, was to have recognised the complexity of the problem involved. His answer to the issue under consideration was accordingly neither single[98] nor simple. As he was among the first to provide a many-sided analysis of the concept of law, we should examine it in detail. If, however, his answers appear obscure or arise from a confusion, we can learn from his mistakes.

Hence my purpose is to elucidate the concept of law by evaluating the pros and cons of Aristotle's views and particularly the terms on which in his eyes a law can be considered valid. As will be seen, he provides *different types* of answer to this question. These must be examined critically, since it is not always possible to pass from one to the other for purposes of corroboration or inference. For example, if the answers given correspond to different senses of 'law' or to different contexts in which the word may be used, then they must be on different logical levels and have a different logical force and implication at each level. A transition from one type of answer to the other might then be tantamount to a category mistake, and accordingly engender paradoxes or inconsistencies.

Since no fully systematic exposition of the concept of law occurs in any of Aristotle's works, one has to assemble the relevant passages from his various writings. If I am correct, there are altogether four headings under which his answers to the question, 'What is the nature of law and the reason for its binding force?' can be conveniently grouped.

1. The General Nature of Law and the Concept of Equity
2. The Rationality of Law
3. The Moral Nature of Law
4. Conservative and Reformative Justice

(The last heading covers the belief in the antiquity of the law and habits of obedience to it on the one hand, and demands for a progressively adjustable law on the other.)

In ancient Greece, a number of additional answers were given to the basic question. There was the assumption that the purpose of validation was best achieved by invoking an alleged decree on the part of some divinity or well-known legislator. Other arguments were that the function of law was to prevent or correct wrongdoing, or alternatively to represent the best of public opinion. At times, it was emphasised that the law embodied a general covenant between members of civil society, or again that it expressed a universal consensus. According to Aristotle, none of these interpretations was acceptable; indeed, in his view they were either irrelevant or involved an acceptance of human liberty to a degree which to him appeared unjustifiable.

The concept Aristotle had in mind under (1) was that of an unwritten natural law.[99] He considered that there might be a law which applied to all men, in all places, and at all times, though perhaps not in all circumstances. In one passage,[100] he speaks of 'absolute justice', which according to Ernest Barker's[101] conjecture means that this form of justice is not relative to any particular community. Absolute justice, therefore, would be justice between man and man *sub specie humanitatis*; as such, it would be distinguishable from justice between citizens *qua* citizens, i.e. political or legal justice.

Of course, to speak of the nature of law as general is ambiguous. I am not thinking now of the ambiguity of the word 'law', i.e. the possible confusion between laws describing the uniformities of nature on the one hand (e.g. to use Aristotle's previously-mentioned example, fire burning alike in Greece and in Persia, both in the past and in the present),[102] and laws prescribing that men should conduct themselves in certain ways on the other. It is worth repeating, however, that this particular confusion is largely due to the fact that believers in a natural moral law have thought that what is *normative* in the proper conduct of men is as readily discoverable by observation and reasoning as are the *regularities* of motions and of other phenomena in nature which are formulated by scientific laws. Rather, the ambiguity I have in mind is that of the word 'general', which may mean common or universally applicable, and also unspecified, vague or indistinct. Since Aristotle does not define his meaning clearly, it is essential for the purpose of my analysis to bear in mind the word's different connotations.[103]

The points which deserve attention are the following. If by 'general' is meant 'applicable to all', a principle of universality is invoked which may support the claim for the universalisability or pervasive validity of moral judgements. By the same token, the word 'general' may refer to the timeless present of certain immutable principles like those in mathematics, or again to anything for which validity without reference to date is claimed. 'General' might then mean universally or eternally true, though for my present purpose I shall not distinguish further between these first two connotations. On the other hand, 'general' may mean that, as Aristotle states, 'the judgement of the legislator does not apply to a particular case, but is universal'.[104] If, as is probable in this quotation, the word 'universal' or 'general' means indeterminate or vague, a characteristic mark of such a generic rule of law lies in the presence of gaps in the area to which it applies or, put differently, in the absence of details and qualifications in its formulation.

It is precisely for this reason that the definition of law as a general rule has often, if not always, recommended itself. The more general the formulation of a rule of law, in the last of my three senses, the more vague it will be, and therefore the greater the freedom of its subjects.[105] Hegel affirmed that in a modern state, dictates of law should stop short at the general and leave its citizens scope to decide the particular means of its fulfilment. For example, if there is a law for the payment of debts or taxes and another for the schooling of every child, the specific form in which debts or taxes are paid or schooling takes place may be left to the discretion of individuals. Again, suppose there is a law enjoining that one should assist one's neighbours. Would it not be up to each individual to determine what sort of assistance is implied in the command, whom one is to consider one's neighbour, or how often the precept is to be carried out? On somewhat similar grounds,[106] and indeed as a result of his acceptance of law as a general rule, Locke introduced the notion of prerogative power, which consists in the right of the chief executive to issue special decrees in an emergency. Laws formulated in general terms might indeed leave undetermined the way in which to deal with unexpected contingencies, and hence call for initiative and *ad hoc* decisions on the part of a ruler. Common to the beliefs of the philosophers I have mentioned is that, in their view, the condition of generality in the law is a prerequisite for the exercise of discretion and liberty, on the part of either ruler or subject. Certainly, one of the aims of traditional liberalism might be defined as the attempt to limit the efficacy of law by keeping it as generic or vaguely formulated as possible. Aristotle was no liberal in the modern sense of the word; nevertheless, the seeds of the liberal tradition might be traced back to his interpretation of the concept of law in the generic sense I have described.

Aristotle's more detailed views on the general nature of law can be expressed in the form of three arguments, one of which is based largely on my first meaning of 'general', while the other two, the more interesting ones, are based mainly on the third meaning. All three arguments might be regarded as replies to objections by an imaginary critic.[107] The conclusion in the case of each argument is that, apart from exceptional instances, the general nature of a law is its prevalent, and indeed its most fundamental, attribute.

The first objection to Aristotle's doctrine is the assertion that a general law is sovereign only to the extent that it is 'rightly constituted', and that the latter qualification is indeed the validating ground for its obligatory nature. Aristotle has two answers to this objection. In the first place, he explains that the phrase 'rightly constituted' remains undefined unless it refers to a common interest or a certain legitimate claim, each of which would involve conditions of generality of some sort. Secondly, in his view, even though a law may depend on a constitution and bind, not because of its generality but because of its constitutional basis, it is most improbable that a constitution would consist of special decrees only, and not also of general rules. Hence generality again appears as one of the basic elements in the nature of a law.

The second objection, a critic might argue, is that precisely because laws are formulated in general terms, personal rule (single or collective) should take the place of legal sovereignty. This argument has always been the stock-in-trade of monarchists and all those favouring personal initiative and governmental power over and against the rule of law. Aristotle replies to this objection by emphasising that a general and authoritative principle of some sort must be present even in the mind of a personal ruler. The concept of law as a general maxim thus remains basic.

Finally, and most significantly (as I shall show later), Aristotle himself concedes that, because of their generic form or vagueness, laws must be changed from time to time; that, especially in their unwritten form (which is bound to be inexact), they should be modified in the light of further experience of particular circumstances and also by what Aristotle calls the principle of equity. By 'equity' he means arbitration;[108] he also has in mind a kind of justice which makes amends for the generality of legal formulae and their disregard of the individual case or possible exceptions to a rule.[109] The admission represents no inconsistency in Aristotle's thought. On the contrary, it expresses a point of both subtlety and importance.

In the first place, principles of equity are valueless if introduced without 'rhyme and reason', i.e. without a moral purpose or some general rule. Secondly – and here I perceive real insight on the part of Aristotle – the generality grounded in the nature of law is as such not superseded or cancelled by the fact that there may be cases containing unforeseen circumstances where the law is silent. His point is that a general rule of law remains valid to the extent that the conditions *to which it applies* are general. Or one might say that though in exceptional cases a given law may not necessarily apply, it does not follow that this law thereby forfeits its basic claim to be observed in all cases which obviously fall under it. There is a parallel here with the principle of equality – another general and vague rule. If a believer in equality concedes that there may be cases where an unequal treatment of men is reasonable or equitable, and therefore imperative – for instance when the elderly are given benefits or a deserving person receives a reward – nobody would insist that such an admission involves a rejection of the primary claim to equality.[110] Indeed, the issue may be formulated in a more radical way. One might say that an exception to a general law *confirms* this law as general, just as an exception to a rule proves the rule.

The point I have in mind is connected with an avoidance of the fallacy of accident or *secundum quid*.[111] This fallacy consists of the error of arguing from a general rule taken without qualification to a special case considered under certain qualifications. Examples of the fallacy are: 'He who thrusts a knife into another person should be punished; a surgeon in operating does so; therefore the surgeon should be punished.' Or: 'The deliberate taking of life is murder; soldiers in war deliberately take life; therefore they are murderers.' The fallacy is avoided if attention is paid to some obvious, though not explicitly stated, conditions that render the general, unqualified rule inapplicable in exceptional cases. In the examples cited, the exceptional cases are those of the surgeon and the soldier. As Eaton explains, 'there are conditions understood, but not expressed, behind every rule; the exceptions make these conditions explicit'. The sense, then, in which the exception to a rule confirms the rule is that the exception exemplifies an implicitly understood limitation upon the otherwise universally valid rule. Similarly, a case of equitable inequality of treatment might be said to exemplify an implicitly understood limitation upon the otherwise universally valid claim for equality, and, in so doing, indirectly to confirm the egalitarian claim.

Likewise, when in Aristotle's terms equity takes the place of a principle of natural justice which is embodied in a general law, the general law as such remains valid. 'Equity', as he puts it, 'covers a gap left uncovered by law proper.'[112] Sometimes the gap in question is predictable, sometimes not. It is not predictable if a legislator finds himself unable to conceive of a perfect rule which fits all cases, but has none the less to formulate a rule applicable in a majority of cases. It is also unpredictable if an infinite number of possible variations makes it difficult for a legislator to lay down a definite rule. In either case, the difficulty lies in specifying in advance an exhaustive list of possible exceptions.

Aristotle's own example is that of making a rule for each size and shape of weapon that may be used for wounding another person (note the resemblance between this and the example cited in illustration of the fallacy of *secundum quid*). If a definite rule to this effect were needed, a legislator (according to Aristotle) would have to express himself in 'unqualified' terms, i.e. he ought to speak of 'any instrument'. As a result, a man who happens to wear a ring when raising his hand against another, and actually but unintentionally strikes him, must present the judge with a dilemma. According to the letter of the law, Aristotle explains, the man is a wrongdoer liable to punishment; but in fact he has done no wrong. Equity, Aristotle infers, is the way in which to deal with this dilemma. It is a correction of the law where the law errs because of its generality. Equity affirms and brings into the open what the legislator himself *would* have ruled, 'had he foreseen that the case might arise'.[113]

The implication again is that equity, by making explicit a qualification intended or understood but not actually expressed in the formulation of a general rule of law, confirms rather than abolishes this rule. While equity represents the 'better sort of justice' in all those cases where the emergence of new features requires justification, the universal rule of law remains 'by its very nature' the standard of justice precisely because it is unable to specify or 'condescend upon particulars'. Hence it is perfectly consistent for Aristotle to define the equitable as 'a correction of law where law is defective owing to its universality', and at the same time to urge that, although 'the law is aware that there is a possibility of error (i.e. in the exceptional case), the fault is not in the law nor in the framer of the law, but in its unwarranted application, i.e. the law itself (as a general rule) remains correct'.[114]

Aristotle has further observations to make about the generality of law which explain how he can pass, to his own satisfaction, from speaking of the law as general to speaking of it as rational. He holds that part, at least, of what is meant by saying that the law is general is that it is unaffected by the emotions and other feelings which influence people's minds, even those of a political ruler, a legislator or a founder of cities. In being impersonal, therefore, the rule of law can claim to be objective and incorruptible; together with 'absolute justice', it is a mean and a neutral authority,[115] like Adam Smith's 'impartial spectator' or a Kantian regulative idea. In this capacity, it may be regarded as a rational standard or a principle of reason.

(vi) THE RATIONAL AND MORAL NATURE OF LAW: CONSERVATIVE AND REFORMATIVE JUSTICE

The emphasis on the rational nature of law, clearly included in Aristotle's exposition, is associated with the assumption that reason can make discoveries, and, if properly employed, lead to the disclosure of principles of absolute or natural justice. Furthermore, there is the suggestion that the idea of law as a law of reason implies that it is possible to justify it rationally, and in fact that its validity can be proved to be necessary and universal.

Altogether, we find two kinds of argument in the context of Aristotle's conception of law as rational.

In the first place, he remarks that the law, presumably both in its making and in its content, proceeds from moral prudence and understanding.[116] This may mean no more than that every rule of law involves a rational principle, or that it is reasonable and unaffected by prejudice. If, on the other hand, a stronger meaning is intended, it might involve acceptance of the Platonic approach to ethics or of the 'intellectualist' theory of law. This is based on the contention that, in Bishop Butler's words, 'there is, in the nature of things, an original standard of right and wrong in actions, independent of all will, but which unalterably determines the will (even) of God'.[117] Since, in a passage already mentioned, Aristotle refers to law as the rule of both God and reason,[118] he could be understood to be aiming at a compromise between the 'voluntarist' and the 'intellectualist' definitions.[119] Throughout, however, he stresses that the rule of law is binding because of its rational nature and its impersonal origin, both of which make its acceptance comparatively easy: unlike personal rule, it cannot be considered either 'burdensome' or a possible 'object of hatred'.

Secondly, Aristotle holds that law 'is a system of order' and that 'order' means purposeful, rational behaviour.[120] He goes on to argue that for the enforcement of the law as a system of order and for the formation of a habit of obedience to it, a general system of 'orderliness' in the state is essential. Such a system, he maintains, can be secured only if certain necessary conditions in the social and economic organisation of a political community are satisfied. One of these would lie in a limited population of, say, less than 100,000 inhabitants. By the same token, the number of citizens ought not to fall, say, below 10. Likewise, the territorial size of a state should not be either too large or too small. If it is too small, the principle of self-sufficiency, on which Aristotle places so much emphasis, could not be secured. That is to say, only on the basis of a certain functional relationship between ends and means can a political association become self-sufficient and preserve a healthy mode of existence directed towards desirable goals. What Aristotle stipulates, therefore, is that a city state should possess its own material resources and not depend on outside help; it should secure full employment and satisfy the need for human development, moral and spiritual as well as material.

There is a parallel here between Aristotle's stipulations for preventing an object from forfeiting its nature (or otherwise becoming functionally defective) and the principles of Minimum Space and Minimum Time laid down by Collingwood[121] as requirements for an understanding of both history and natural science. Collingwood's point is that every event or fact presupposes the existence of a minimum amount of time in order to be able to occur. Just as at least two people are needed to make up a game of tennis or to start a quarrel, and three to incite jealousy, so at least several seconds are necessary for a process of walking to materialise, a day or two for painting a picture, two months for learning to type, several years for founding an empire, and a whole lifetime, at least on Aristotle's view, for achieving happiness.

Aristotle explains that there is also a maximum limit to the establishment of a system of 'orderliness': the city state must not be too large. Inordinate size will render it 'unwieldy' and 'unsurveyable'; it will cease to be within the easy command of a general (as though the giving of orders presupposed being within earshot of one's fellow citizens or having a stentorian voice!).[122] Certainly, in a large community, spies and law-breakers might escape detection and, most important of all, it would be far more difficult to defend a state from outside aggression and to maintain a 'way of life', based as this is on a workable constitution and a genuine system of order. The consequence is that, in the absence of either form of order, i.e. either without self-sufficiency or without a constitution, it will be difficult to enforce the law which is itself an order.

What, then, is one to make of this argument, if indeed it is an argument? As I see it, there are four ways of interpretation, only the last of which appears to me acceptable.

Aristotle may mean that there is a correlation between quantitative or material determinations of politics on the one hand and qualitative or spiritual conditions of political life on the other. If this is his meaning, the correlation might in the last resort be between factual statements such as occur in economics or geography, and value judgements such as arise in ethics and the language of legal obligation. This correlation would be unacceptable to those who draw a line between facts and norms, description and prescription. Secondly, Aristotle may regard the proposition 'if there are at least a few laws and a general habit of obedience to these laws in a given community, then a system of orderliness and a "way of life" exist in that community' as a mere tautology. It is clear, however, that the statement quoted is in a logically different class from, say, 'if x is a brother, then x is male'. In other words, one can accept the assertion that certain enforceable laws exist in a given community and yet deny that either a way of life or a system of orderliness in Aristotle's sense prevail in that community. Thirdly, Aristotle might conceive of the sovereign rule of law as a system of order by an analogy with nature and from the argument for unity: every multiplicity, in order to become one harmonious whole, requires some unitary or single principle governing it, 'just as what is hot is best suited to heat things'.[123] The analogy is not compelling and, besides, involves the use of the two ambiguous words 'unity' and 'oneness', which may mean either singleness or coherence of parts.

Finally, Aristotle's purpose may be to offer an *analysis* of the concept of law as a system of order. This can be illustrated from a consideration of another concept, such as anger. For instance, it might be argued that this concept cannot be properly employed unless the following three conditions are satisfied: a person other than the angered person must be involved; that person must be causing harm; in so doing, he must act intentionally.[124] Similarly, in his analysis of law as an order, Aristotle might distinguish three conditions which, in his view, are presupposed by the meaningful use of the word 'law'. He might stipulate that unless a state (besides incorporating a 'way of life') is also self-sufficient and has a moderately-sized population, there can be no law as a system of order in that state, nor *a fortiori* a habit of obedience to such a law. I believe that, if Aristotle's doctrine is understood in this way, it becomes more intelligible than if interpreted otherwise; it also leaves scope for genuine argument. For instance, just as the meaningful use of the concept of anger might survive the elimination of one or other of the conditions which I have cited as necessary for its application, so it might remain true to say that the concept of law as a system of order presupposes, among other things, the element of self-sufficiency – though not perhaps that of limited size with regard to either population or territory.

From his notion of the rule of law as rational and as a system of order, Aristotle would have considered it possible to pass to the idea that the purpose of law is moral: it promotes human virtue and, above all, it serves the common interest.

The transition is tempting, especially because 'rational' can itself be used as a normative term. In some sense, it would be odd to say 'the rational thing for you to do is to do *x*, but you ought not to do *x*'. On the other hand, one of the difficulties in the tradiditional doctrine of a moral law as a law of reason is the equation of moral values with rational validity. Indeed, it is notoriously problematic to argue that either human reason or any process of rational justification can become a self-depending source of moral obligation.

The task to which I propose to confine myself is that of clarifying further the sense in which Aristotle can be considered a natural-law theorist rather than a legal positivist. If, to quote H. L. A. Hart,[125] we understand by legal positivism 'the simple contention that it is in no sense a necessary truth that laws reproduce or satisfy certain demands of morality', Aristotle can be shown to advocate the opposite of such a contention. A few examples may illustrate this. He holds that no municipal law could act against a person pre-eminently superior in goodness, 'like a god among men'.[126] Indeed, in his opinion, since such a person would be a law unto himself, he could not be accepted as part of a civil state. I think Aristotle would have regarded the word 'could' in the last two sentences as having logical force and not just a purely matter-of-fact meaning. Elsewhere, as we have seen, he distinguishes between two senses of the phrase 'rule of law'.[127] One is where obedience is expected to such laws as have been enacted; another, where obedience is required to laws which have been *well* enacted. Since it is possible to pay obedience to badly-enacted laws, it is clear where Aristotle's preference lies. Similarly, having taken note of his view that among well-enacted laws some are the best relative to the men obeying them, while others are absolutely and universally the best, we must again recognise that Aristotle's preference is for the second type of law. His reason for the choice would be that the concept of law implies (a) justice, (b) moral purpose and (c) general validity, all of which differ from self-interest and a merely conventional legality. In one passage,[128] in fact, he expressly states that the better a man is, the more he will affirm and make use of laws which are unwritten and which form part of the unchanging, universal law of nature.

The one sense, according to Aristotle, in which the connection between law and moral principles breaks down is when iniquitous laws are enacted, which may in turn give rise to a conflict of obedience in the people facing these bad legal rules who also acknowledge the basic requirements of morality. Besides, one might argue independently of Aristotle that, though justice is a most important part of ethics, it is possible to speak of it in a purely legal context, regardless of moral values or ethical concepts. Compulsory school education, taxation and national insurance may be vindicated in accordance with the principles of distributive justice, without introducing any of the specific criteria of moral evaluation, except perhaps such vague notions as the 'public interest'. Even the latter concept, depending as it does on interpretation, may vary from one constitution, society or government to another, and may in effect be linked with oppressive or aggressive policies. Furthermore, a case can be made for drawing hard and fast lines of demarcation between legal rules and legal obligation on the one hand, and moral rules and moral obligation on the other. Though there may be, at all times and in all places, a partial overlap in content and terminology between ethics and the law, the distinction between them is not unlike that between 'internal' moral factors such as deliberation, intention, voluntariness, integrity, personal autonomy, conscience, guilt or remorse on the one hand, and open acts of legislation, judicial hearings, or threats of physical penalties for breaches of the law on the other.[129]

In all other respects, it must be admitted, there are important connections between morality and the law: hence Aristotle was, without doubt, entitled to regard the two as partially coextensive. However, the question of whether a legally valid system must *necessarily* conform to ethical demands requires careful scrutiny and may remain an open issue. Perhaps the most that can be said, if one were to answer the question affirmatively and in present-day terms, is that natural-law theorists ought first of all to limit their aspirations by reformulating their views without ambiguity and in mainly secular terms, together with a minimum of content and fixed claims. In this case, the more realisable these provisos are, the greater is the possibility of arguing that law and morality have of necessity some elementary truths and some basic rules of obligation in common.

We come now to the last topic for discussion in this section. Aristotle lays strong emphasis in his legal doctrine on the idea of a time-honoured origin of laws and on habit as a basis for validating these laws: 'Law derives its validity from habit upon which obedience is founded. But habit can be created only by the passage of time.'[130]

Here, the existence of a 'customary morality' is assumed, with other philosophers joining Aristotle in arguing that on certain grounds what is traditional must also be morally good. Burke and Hume maintained this no less than the Romans, who vigorously advocated the obligations of ancestral traditions: 'mos maiorum'. Customary morality is largely identical with habitual behaviour in a social group. And just as custom has been considered sacred, with its practices exercising coercive power universally, so has habit been regarded by many as an obligatory force at all times. One of the reasons behind the belief that both customary and habitual forms of behaviour correspond to rules of compelling force is that any divergence from group habits tends to meet with disapproval, social pressure for conformity, or, indeed, outright hostility. International law is in part customary, and the sanctions behind it are similarly based on the likelihood of an organised and hostile reaction to deviations.

If one wanted to distinguish between habit and custom, one might do so by regarding habit as an embodiment of popular opinion and conduct in a given place and at a particular time, whereas custom would represent something more elemental and 'natural', or, in a word, universal, either in the geographical or in the historical sense. English Common Law, as interpreted by Sir Edward Coke in his controversy with James I and Francis Bacon, is a clear example of the way in which a whole body of law can be assumed to be grounded in custom and tradition, 'refined and perfected by all the wisest men in former succession of ages, and proved and approved by continual experience'.[131] The fundamental significance of common law, in Coke's view, lay in its ability to limit decisively the king's authority and even that of parliament. He thought that some of the authoritative nature and compelling force of common law resided in the fact that it was 'given' and 'cannot but with great hazard and danger be altered and changed'. Aristotle's notion of the antiquity and customary nature of law represents an early and prominent anticipation of issues such as these. However, quite justifiably, his doctrine falls into two parts, one in favour of tradition and customary rules of law, the other in defence of progress and corresponding changes in the law.[132]

On the one hand, he considers laws founded on unwritten custom more sovereign than those which have been written down; he also believes that the former are concerned with questions of greater importance.[133] Besides, in his view, there is nothing to be gained from the very best of laws, unless one can ensure the stability of a constitution. Accordingly, citizens should be trained by force of habit in the right constitutional temper.[134] It follows that (a) in order to cultivate habits fairly long periods of time are required; and (b) customary rules of law must have been in existence and have remained unaltered ever since remote antiquity. Habit formation certainly occupies a decisive place in Aristotle's theory of education. He regards every settled habit as something like 'second nature', placed as it were between reason and nature as one of the three factors which render men virtuous. One could argue then that, according to him, laws inculcate habits which in their turn enable men to practise virtue. Alternatively, in order to achieve their effect, laws necessarily presuppose a process of habituation from which they derive their power to command obedience and respect. In either case, on Aristotle's principles, any change in law must constitute a defect and particularly a risk: it might even lead to a weakening of the power of the law. In one passage,[135] therefore, he goes so far as to equate 'the system followed in ancient times' with 'the natural system', and this with 'the standard of absolute justice' which must always be adhered to.

On the other hand, thinking along progressive lines, Aristotle recognises that customs express human desires and, if the latter change, the former may have to be altered as well.[136] Indeed, he admits that customs *develop* to the same extent as a political community progresses towards its natural 'form'. Changes in the law would therefore be natural and binding, just as the development of an organism is natural and, in a sense, normative. Besides, neither written nor unwritten laws might be sufficiently relevant or determinate for application in every new case or matter of detail: 'rules must be expressed in general terms, but actions are concerned with particulars'. Hence, modification of the law should sometimes be necessary in the light of changing circumstances, and also, as we have seen earlier, in order to do justice to the claims of equity. Aristotle has especially in mind the constant need to prepare for changes brought about by circumstances beyond human control; whenever these occur, one has to adjust as rapidly as possible and often by *ad hoc* decision.

The merits of Aristotle's 'traditionalist' approach are these.

1. He realises that some rules of law, in almost every legal system, originate in custom – either replacing or strengthening it, according to the attitude of the legislator.
2. He recognises that not all laws are necessarily enacted, and that they are not all the expression of conscious thought.
3. He is able to explain and substantiate the rationale of a habit of obedience on the part of legal subjects and of the resulting continuity of both laws and the law-making power.

Aristotle's 'traditionalist' attitude has two defects, or conversely his 'progressive' policy of advocating occasional changes in the law has two merits. He acknowledges that just as habits are not in themselves normative and traditions are not self-justifying, so neither of them can ultimately constitute obligations or confer rights. If, then, habitual regularities of behaviour are not necessarily standards of correct conduct, the way is open, at least on certain occasions, for justifying the abolition of old laws and the adoption of new ones. Secondly, the assumption that either moral or legal standards are universally and permanently valid is difficult to substantiate. We are all aware that the different social, cultural, or religious backgrounds of a particular community can give rise to different ethical standards within that community at any given time (e.g. in modern times in connection with such issues as divorce, abortion, euthanasia or capital punishment). Similarly, if moral needs were to change from one generation to another, would this not bring about a diversity of outlook and, consequently, the substitution of new laws for old? As Benn and Peters observe,[137] some traditionalists like Burke have argued that the survival of a legal order is evidence that it satisfies a nation's moral needs. But suppose that these moral needs fail to be satisfied. Surely, on Burke's own premises, this should be sufficient grounds for concluding that a change in the given order is justified.

5 Summary and Conclusion

These then are the main strands in Aristotle's conception of law. The analysis I have attempted seems to me to reflect Aristotle's views on the complex nature of law and the different grounds for its validity. I think that the several aspects of his doctrine are not ultimately related, and that there is no necessary conflict between them, since most embody answers to different questions concerning the law. The recurrent theme of my own comments has been the assumption that 'law' is a complex term, comprising in its application a number of different definitions in relation to rules and validity, authority and obligation, sources of law and stages of its evolution, and the like. In my opinion, it is a merit of Aristotle's theory that he appears to recognise the multiple meaning of the word and, accordingly, the need for a multiple definition.

There are, however, a number of issues which he leaves unsatisfactorily vague. To the extent that he advances, in a rudimentary form, the notion that laws are fundamentally general and rational, he can be held responsible for some of the confusions inherent in the traditional concept of a law of nature.[1] Certain terms he uses, such as 'general', 'universal' and 'rational', are clearly ambiguous. Again, though his views on the indeterminate character of the law are undoubtedly important, his fusion of different meanings of 'general' or 'rational', and the transition from one *kind* of discourse to another which such a fusion invites, constitute a trap for the unwary. For instance, does 'rational', if applied to law, mean that the contents of the law are discernible by reason, that they are demonstrable by reason, or again that they embody a set of timeless rational truths and values? Aristotle might have accepted one or another, and possibly all three of these different meanings, though none of them, I believe, would be altogether acceptable to anyone today.

Moreover, the discovery of a rational, uniform pattern of human behaviour and the description of resistance to deviations from such a uniformity of conduct do not, in themselves, indicate the existence of an overall prescriptive 'law of nature'. Neither need one accept the close relationship between the rational and the moral aspects of the concept of law in Aristotle's doctrine. Perhaps his greatest misconception is the claim that laws of proper conduct (i.e. laws *requiring* men to behave in certain ways) are like laws *formulating* (not really 'governing') the regularities of nature, and that both may be ascertained by rational inference. Besides, at times Aristotle fails to distinguish clearly between logical proof and the necessitation associated with moral obligation. Similarly, there is a crucial difference between the conclusion of a chain of deductive reasoning and a legal decision arrived at according to a rule and in the light of certain evidence. Even if it is assumed that there are rules of law or ethics which are axiomatic in that they supply a general criterion for all legal or moral duties, it is by no means obvious that these would be axiomatic in the same sense as principles of logic or mathematics. But there is not only failure on Aristotle's part to distinguish clearly between descriptive and prescriptive laws and between logical and moral validity. He also tends to blur the distinction between legal and moral validity and to assimilate moral with customary or coercive rules. Yet to ask the question 'Why ought people to obey the law?' is different from demanding, 'What conditions must be satisfied for a rule to be a valid part of a legal system?'[2] Moreover, both these questions are logically independent of the question 'Is the motive for obeying a law the fear that penalties will follow any non-observance of its rules?' It would be yet another confusion to say that the validity of law is the same as its 'efficacy', i.e. the fact that a legal order or a particular rule within that order is obeyed more often than not.[3]

Furthermore, consider Aristotle's assertion of the desirability of ancient and stable laws and his insistence on habits of obedience on the one hand, and his arguments for the modification or even total replacement of either customary or imprecise rules of law on the other. If *combined*, his thoughts have much to offer. They have provided the basis for what is sometimes referred to as 'a theory of natural law with minimum and variable content'. Such a theory would incorporate rules which are general but not static in meaning, and which could therefore be variously applied or interpreted in different contexts. Similarly, though these rules might be in some sense discernible by reason, they should at all times leave room for further reflection and a wide exercise of discretion, even to the point where they might have to be repealed in certain cases. To make provision for such a flexible body of rules would render the notion of the development of a legal system not only more plausible but also justifiable. To say, however, that changes in the law are of the nature of law and can as such be explained, appreciated and even justified is one thing; to affirm that they embody norms prescribing how men ought to develop or how they should perfect their behaviour is another, very different thing. With his teleology, particularly his assimilation of politics and law to principles of moral purpose, Aristotle might have wished to urge the importance of the evaluative if not the prescriptive aspect of this issue. On the other hand, the difference between the two kinds of statement involved, the explanatory and the prescriptive, would have been almost non-existent for him. For this and the other reasons I have mentioned, one might once more part company with Aristotle, in spite of the relevance of his ideas about the reasonableness of substituting new laws for old.

Throughout his discussion, Aristotle rightly conforms to the principle of specification or, in Locke's words, 'distinctly weighs'[4] some of the aspects that constitute the multiple meaning of 'law'. But then, after construing the word as a general principle, certified by reason, and associated with moral purpose and custom, he allows these diverse aspects to merge. As I have tried to show, this is as fallacious as to maintain that, if one of the different ways of construing the word is accepted, this necessarily entails rejecting the others. Just as each meaning of the word can live and survive in its own context, separately from the rest, none is more relevant or 'essential' than any of the others. In fact, Aristotle's different analyses of 'law', in modern perspective, neither exclude nor imply one another. Whatever their merits or shortcomings, this is probably the chief moral to be drawn by us today.

It remains for me to explain the relationship in Aristotle's thought between the notions of conventional and natural law on the one hand and those of justice and equality on the other.

For him, as for many other theorists, the concept of equality is in some sense central to the idea of justice. At the same time, rather than adhere to the principle of strict equality, he perceives the relevance of the rule that people and their affairs are sometimes similar and sometimes different, and that it would therefore be just to treat like cases alike, but unlike cases differently. Hence, according to him, to advocate fairness is not the same as to advocate equality; neither need equitable shares be equal ones. This emphasis on equity is given expression in Aristotle's principle of proportionate equality, and in his view that if an inequality of treatment is required on reasonable or otherwise relevant grounds, it ought to be considered fair and just.

If, then, the notion of equality should sometimes give way to that of equity on the one hand and to the factor of difference on the other, it is still possible for it to survive as the rationale of moral evaluation in either context. In the former, even at the risk of circularity, equality may emerge as the ultimate criterion in attempts to justify some preferential but equitable treatment (as when the elderly or needy are granted advantages which restore to them a certain equality of status and opportunity with the young or the affluent). In the latter context, the fact that there may be social or economic inequality between different classes of people, and between their capacities, status and achievements as citizens, may favour, rather than inhibit, attempts at equalisation between them in some more fundamental respect. However, once the principle of discrimination is accepted on moral or factual grounds, any endeavour to equalise one *sort* of person with another must constitute a problem. For if the differences between people or their attainments are differences of kind rather than of degree, or give rise to even more categorial distinctions, the process of equalisation cannot advance very far or without serious difficulties.

In order to keep control over this question in the direction of either justifying differentiation or attempting equalisation, two procedures can be adopted, one practical, the other theoretical. Recourse to *revolutionary* methods is one option when either the political or the legal stability of a country is undermined, or when the moderating influence of a strong middle class is lacking. The settling of controversies on a *legal* basis finds support when there is room for argument, or when either custom or precedent helps to determine the issue.

The appeal to the law may take the form of deciding questions concerning equality or inequality in the light of the conventional moral or legal codes laid down for this purpose in various political communities at various times. Alternatively, it may take the form of seeking confirmation for a particular decision by recourse to the alleged principles of natural or 'absolute' justice, beyond the partialities of conventional rules. Aristotle favours an appeal to the law in either form, but especially that to a universal law of nature. For he considers that all political issues, including the question of the supreme authority in the state, must be subordinate to the maxim that no person or body of persons, but only law as a general, impartial principle, should be ultimately sovereign. One of the reasons recommending this maxim is that both the established and the developing features of social justice are best served if the rule of law as such combines within itself conservative as well as reformative principles. But the case for the supremacy of a universal, rational law is based, above all, on the need for valid criteria justifying either equal or unequal treatment of men in any given set of circumstances. Aristotle's concept of law as a neutral and impersonal moral arbiter satisfies this function at least in principle, and serves as a preferable alternative to the application of revolutionary methods of decision. But, understandably, his view throughout is that both in theory and in practice it is often very difficult to establish the truth in matters of equality and justice.

I have expressed misgivings about some of the points Aristotle raises in connection with his ideas of law and equality. Still, the main trend of his argument as advanced in various passages of his work appears to me significant and sound, though from a modern point of view it may not satisfy everyone to the same degree. What appeals to me especially, besides the interplay in his thought between general argument and judicious reasoning on practical questions, is his search for a connected theory of the concepts of justice, equality and equitable inequality. His discrimination between the different elements of a political community, among them the all-important differences of kind, appears to me particularly valuable. Part of his genius, one might say, lies in his perception of differences and alternatives, and in fact of whole ranges and levels of possible distinctions. His reflections on the strict as well as the wider application of the term 'equal' are, I think, of fundamental relevance, for they provide a basis from which to assess the merits and the demerits of his own doctrine. They show that equality in a body politic can be established only within the confines of a given social position or professional function, and not between its different kinds throughout the whole of society. They also make clear (though perhaps not altogether to Aristotle himself) that if offices in a state and its various social classes are assumed to differ from one another in relative *importance* and hence in the quality of their contributions to the common interest, then such graded evaluation must necessarily raise the question of the degree of bias in his own principle of proportionate equality. His final and, indeed, very plausible move is to explain that in all controversial cases the only recourse, apart from argument or mathematical calculi, is to revolution on the one hand or to the law on the other.

But, how, it may be asked, can either rebellion or the rule of law promote the implementation of fair egalitarian claims which give due weight to differences and legitimate discrimination? Revolutionary change, unless it is no more than seditious agitation, opposition between factions, or a mere tendency towards innovation, may encourage demands for either equality or equitable inequality between people by forcing the abandonment of unjust methods of treating men and distributing goods. But then, as the expression of political conflict, revolutionary action indicates how controversial the *interpretation* of the public interest, of lawfulness, equity and equality, can become. It is largely for this reason that Aristotle places so much reliance on binding agreements between contesting parties and, in the last resort, on a valid and enforceable law.

Conventional law has the advantage of promoting the interests of social justice by flexible and *ad hoc* decisions in favour of claims to equality which are just and in opposition to those which are not, thereby benefiting both democrats and oligarchs. Also, in determining the nature of commercial dealings and the rights and duties implicit in political negotiations, it advances mutual understanding and an adjustment between the parties involved. Conventional legislative measures can go even further in their support of moderation, justice and equality. They may regulate human desires and the extent of private property; they can formulate principles of punishment; and they can lay down not only that people should rule in turn, but that supreme power should be vested in the municipal law or in a number of men rather than in a single person. Additional benefits can be derived from legal enactment if this enables the middle class to take upon itself the role of arbitrator and guardian of an evenly balanced constitution. Moreover, positive laws are capable of either substantiating or 'correcting' the largely vague rules of natural justice. Finally, though it may be altered or abolished, a civil code of law is enforceable while in being, thereby strengthening people's confidence and their sense of security.

In addition to his remarks about the importance of obedience to the civil law, Aristotle stresses the significance of the obligatory character of a universal law of nature. The relevance of this for his arguments about justice and equality still requires clarification.

In his opinion, claims on behalf of natural justice have objective validity and are binding on men irrespective of the varying conventions peculiar to each state and each period in history. In this type of argument, law is identified with a set of principles which are common and in a sense universalisable. Now, Aristotle's stipulation that each person should receive his due on the basis of the principle of proportionate equality expresses a similar, universalisable, axiom. This is that the ratio between recognition and desert in any one case under consideration should be the same as the ratio in every other. Next, Aristotle speaks of the need to qualify or supplement the rules of justice by making allowance for an unequal treatment of men if, on some ground or other, this is equitable. It follows that Aristotle's reasons for regarding the precepts of natural law as valid are similar to his criteria for looking upon an equal treatment of men as just and on some unequal forms of treatment as fair, namely the explicit rationality, morality and impartiality of the evaluations involved. Furthermore, in his opinion, the validity of laws is based partly on their customary nature and partly on demands made by new progressive movements in political life. This balanced assessment (which combines a conservative with a reformative policy) is in keeping with his view that a citizen's sense for the legality of treating men alike (in some respects at least) depends on habit-formation and long traditions of moral training, just as the appreciation of the fairness of differences in their treatment is derived from new forms of experience and changing social standards.

An important aspect, then, of Aristotle's concept of natural law as a universal rational principle is that it sets the standard on which the theory and practice of a fair and egalitarian political philosophy can be modelled. Certainly, in his view, the 'art' of political justice should seek to impose a system of equality upon the often unjustified inequalities of life in society; and it should aim at instituting equitable and relevant methods of discrimination between men as opposed to their more basic natural differences. Aristotle would like to see these endeavours realised by legislative wisdom, particularly in the form of a constitution inspired by higher-order rules of justice.[5] As we have seen, there are systematic difficulties (even for Aristotle) in establishing an overall equality between social classes, between the diverse functions of the citizens of a state, and between the different kinds of contribution towards its well-being. To the extent that on occasions he seeks to have these difficulties removed, or at least glossed over, there is an inconsistency in his doctrine – especially between his strict scientific and metaphysical views on equality on the one hand and his more flexible political ones on the other.

After all, the crucial point to be stressed is that Aristotle's views on equality, in his politics no less than in his scientific and metaphysical theories, occur in close connection with, and sometimes in sharp contrast to, his concept of difference. In conclusion, therefore, we must examine the exact meaning of this concept at the three levels where it appears in Aristotle's discourse, both as part of the logic of his argument and in the context of his descriptive accounts of civil society.

First, then, in Aristotle's opinion, whenever the principle of proportionate equality is under consideration, the necessity for differentiating between the deserving and the undeserving has to be taken into account. So long as the ratio between reward and merit remains the same for all, there must be unavoidable differences between individuals who contribute more and those who contribute less to the well-being of a state. On this basis, it is not only desirable but eminently reasonable and just if people's shares in political recognition are not always necessarily equal. Hence Aristotle affirms (and I believe rightly) that differentiation and precedence in matters of distributive justice can be as equitable as sameness and equality.

Secondly, in the light of both his strict and his wider definition of equality, he considers it a logical mistake to attempt an equalisation between things which differ in kind. His argument is that there are ultimate differences not only between separate species or categories in either the physical or the logical sense, but also between social classes or the functions of several types of citizen – the 'parts' of a state – in the political sense. While he suggests ways in which the difficulty in equalising these differences may be lessened, he is aware that a permanent problem remains, though, he believes, this may sometimes be resolved (if only on a temporary or partial basis) by legislative measures.

Nevertheless, the existence of a basic problem of equalising the different is one of Aristotle's main discoveries. It is understandable, therefore, that he tends to vacillate between attempts to establish principles of equality on the one hand, and recognising the existence and fundamental importance of categorial differences on the other. One can also explain that, on his view, any search for pervasive equalities across the borderlines of the generically different is bound to fail. Hence, too, on his premises, no equality can be set up in the social sphere as long as differences of kind prevail either between the several elements, parts and classes of a state, or between the diverse forms of life and modes of excellence achieved by individual citizens or the leading political parties. Two further corollaries, both on the logical plane and as a result of Aristotle's factual analyses, are that (a) equalities require a context, either a narrow and specific one, or one determined by a general topic, a category, or a still broader scope of inquiry; and (b) any equality established within a given domain of interest or a given aspect of human life must differ in meaning from that established within any other field of discourse or activity.

Finally, a premise of Aristotelian (and to a certain extent of all except egalitarian) political thinking is that there are not only diversities of kind between people's capacities, interests or achievements, but also different scales of importance for the various social, cultural and economic strata in human life. The egalitarian, naturally, would assert that such hierarchical discrimination between people, and indeed entire classes of people, is iniquitous: that it is just as unwarranted to give special rewards to spacemen and ballet dancers (as is probably the case in the Soviet Union) as it is to allocate distinctive emoluments to company directors and television magnates (as happens in capitalist countries). At times, Aristotle appears to make the most of the idea of differential rewards in the context of a comprehensive method of grading and evaluation. His principle of proportionate equality would then have to apply uniformly to all different kinds of trade and profession in society, in ascending order of their rank and public merit. On these premises, a dustman, naval rating or miner could never hope to attain the recognition bestowed on a physician, admiral or judge. At other times, Aristotle is aware of both the social injustice and particularly the category mistake which such a procedure entails. At this stage of his argument, he holds that there are various measures whereby equality can be *imposed* upon people who are unfairly discriminated against as a result of the low assessment of their value or usefulness as citizens – either in some form of public pressure or (if principles of equity and law fail altogether) by active resistance. However, in his opinion, these methods in turn can be justified only in exceptional circumstances. One of the central issues of political argument for Aristotle as well as for Locke and for present-day radicals is whether existing systems of law and of society are to remain valid, or whether revolution and new principles of social equality are justifiable.

Appendix

(Page 38, note 35)

In his discussion of the relationship between the one and the equal,[1] Aristotle's comments are more explicit. He observes that, since each concept has a contrary and the idea of the one is opposed to that of the many, the equal must be opposed to the greater or less. As I noted above,[2] in the light of Russell's pertinent views on this issue, Aristotle is incorrect in treating the equal as the opposite of the greater or less, since the equal is the opposite of the unequal and refers to quantities, whereas the greater or less is opposed to sameness and applies to magnitudes. Thus while two quantities (e.g. two rulers) are equal if they have the same magnitude, they are unequal if the one is greater and the other less in magnitude. Aristotle is partially aware of his mistake, for he is puzzled to find that the equal is opposed not only to the greater or less but also to the unequal. Nevertheless, we should consider the development of his argument. He proceeds to question whether the equal, in being contrary to the greater or less, is contrary (a) to the greater alone, (b) to the less alone, or (c) to both in conjunction. He decides that its opposition is not to (a), (b) or (c), since it cannot be the opposite of the greater rather than the less or of the less rather than the greater, nor of more things than one. Neither can it be intermediate between the great and the small (i.e. differing from them in degree only), for no contrary is, either empirically or logically speaking, intermediate between what it is opposed to: otherwise it would not be a perfect contrary. Aristotle's conclusion is that the equal is the privation (or absence) of the greater and the less, though not a necessary privation; for not everything which is neither greater nor less is equal, but only those things which can be either greater or less. The equal, then, is what is neither great nor small, but is by nature so qualified as to become either the one or the other; in this sense, it can be said to be intermediate between the two. For in being neither greater nor

116

less, but opposed to both as a privative negation, it stands for something complete in itself.

After resolving his difficulties concerning the logical status of the equal in this manner, Aristotle mentions the good and the bad, which (as we have seen)[3] are likewise 'dimension words' and are therefore found in every category. On the analogy of his remarks about the equal, he states that what is neither good nor bad is opposed to both. However, unlike the equal, this privative contradiction of both the good and the bad has no name of its own. Aristotle's explanation for this fact is that the good and the bad have several meanings in accordance with the several categories in which they are found, and therefore have no one appropriate subject matter. This observation may indicate that in his opinion, since there is a name for the opposite of the greater or less, i.e. the equal, neither the greater or less nor the equal has several meanings and therefore cannot be found in more than one of the various categories. However, such an inference seems to be invalid. For one thing, the fact that the good and the bad admit of several senses does not appear to account sufficiently for the absence of a name for their opposite. Secondly, Aristotle follows up his consideration concerning the opposite of the good and the bad by remarking that not even that which is neither white nor black has one name, and the reason for this is most certainly not that any of the colour words has several meanings – for none has.

Notes

Notes to Chapter 1: Proportionate Equality and Social Class

1. In the *Laws*, Bk V, 744 B, Plato suggests that in the proportionate distribution of offices or honours regard should be had to a man's 'due' qualifications, including his bodily strength and beauty. For Aristotle's criticism of such a view see his *Politics*, Bk III, 1282 b 23–30; 1283 a 4–11.

2. For anticipations in Plato, particularly the *Republic* and the *Laws*, see Karl R. Popper, *The Open Society and Its Enemies* (London, 1945; 4th rev. edn, 1962) vol. I, ch. 6, and notes 9 (pp. 248ff.) and 20 (pp. 256ff.). See also Ernest Barker, *Greek Political Theory* (London, 1918; 3rd edn, 1947) pp. 334–5 and *passim*, and his *The Political Thought of Plato and Aristotle* (London, 1906; Dover edn, New York, 1959) pp. 196ff.

3. For these two points see *Nicomachean Ethics*, Bk V, ch. i, 1129 a and b. See also F. Rosen, 'The Political Context of Aristotle's Categories of Justice', *Phronesis*, XX (1975), and the literature cited there; also D. D. Raphael, *Justice and Liberty* (London, 1980) pp. 76, 80–1.

4. *The Politics of Aristotle*, trans. with an Introduction, Notes and Appendices by Ernest Barker (Oxford, 1946) Bk III, chs ix, xii, xiii. My references throughout are to this edition, though some of the translations of the Greek text quoted in the present work are my own.

5. Ch. Perelman, *The Idea of Justice and the Problem of Argument* (London, 1963) chs i, iii, v, vii.

6. For two modern analyses of the interrelation of justice with equality and of the principles of an egalitarian justice which accepts as just certain claims of unequal treatment see William K. Frankena, 'The Concept of Social Justice', and Gregory Vlastos, 'Justice and Equality', in Richard B. Brandt (ed.), *Social Justice* (Englewood Cliffs, N. J., 1962).

7. For proportionate and numerical equality see also *Politics*, Bk V, ch. i, sects 12–15. The Aristotelian idea of proportionate equality has survived in the second of two different formulations of the right to equality which present-day citizens hold. 'The first is the right to *equal treatment*, which is the right to an equal distribution of some opportunity or resource or burden. Every citizen, for example, has a

118

right to an equal vote in a democracy. .... The second is the right to *treatment as an equal*, which is the right, not to receive the same distribution of some burden or benefit, but to be treated with the same respect and concern as anyone else. ... The right to treatment as an equal is fundamental, and the right to equal treatment, derivative. In some circumstances the right to treatment as an equal will entail a right to equal treatment, but not, by any means, in all circumstances' (Ronald Dworkin, *Taking Rights Seriously* (London, 1977) p. 227, also p. 273). The fundamental right to treatment as an equal will therefore depend on the sovereign question of political theory, i.e. the question of what inequalities in goods, opportunities and liberties are permitted in a state supposed to be governed by the liberal conception of equality, and why.

8. As Richard Robinson rightly observes, Aristotle in Book III, Chapter ix, refers 'to the wide and vague claims of equality often made in political argument ... indicating how in his opinion they require to be limited and specified' (*Aristotle's Politics, Books III and IV*, translated with Introduction and Comments (Oxford, 1962) p. 33).

9. For the moral connotation see the golden rule (*Matt.* VII, 12), and for the aesthetic one, the golden section of a line (Euclid, *Elements*, II, 11). For the 'sentimental' appeal of egalitarianism, see Popper, *Open Society*, vol. I, p. 96. In the *Politics*, Bk III, ch. xiii, sects 13–15, 20–2, Aristotle equates equality and political justice with the rules of symmetry and proportion.

10. This, so far as I have observed, is always quoted without a reference. The reason seems obvious. Though Mill, in Chapter V of his *Utilitarianism*, refers to it as 'Bentham's dictum' and quotes it in inverted commas, the formula as such does not form part of anything Bentham wrote either in print or in manuscript.

11. James Harrington, *Oceana* (London, 1747; ed. J. Toland) pp. 47–8.

12. H. Khatchadourian, 'Vagueness', *The Philosophical Quarterly*, 12 (1962) 148. For the view that 'the central argument for equality is a muddle' see J. R. Lucas, 'Against Equality', *Philosophy*, XL (1965). For a more recent attempt to analyse the ambiguity and inadequacy of several egalitarian formulae see N. E. Bowie, 'Equality and Distributive Justice', *Philosophy*, XLV (1970).

13. Douglas Jay, *Socialism in the New Society* (London, 1962) p. 4.

14. *Institutiones*, Bk I, tit. i, para. 3, p. 1 (ed. P. Krueger); also *Digesta*, Bk I, tit. i, para. 10, p. 1 (ed. T. Mommsen), in *Corpus Iuris Civilis* (Berlin, 1872) vol. I. See also Cicero, *De Legibus*, Bk I, ch. vi, sect. 19.

15. Cf. H. Kelsen, *General Theory of Law and State* (Harvard, 1949) pp. 9–10, 439.

16. For the vast range of meanings of the word 'freedom' and the fact that

it is therefore not a uniquely descriptive word see Maurice Cranston, *Freedom: A New Analysis* (London, 1953) pt I.

17. For a formal and more detailed treatment see below, ch. 2, sect. ii, paras 9–12.

18. Rousseau, *The Social Contract* (1762) Bk I, ch. i, opening line.

19. Sect. 61, line 1; see also sect. 119, line 1. References are to Peter Laslett's edition of Locke's *Two Treatises of Government* (Cambridge, amended 2nd edn, 1970).

20. Ibid., sect. 87, lines 1–2.

21. See Matthew Arnold, 'Equality', in *Poetry and Prose, Mixed Essays*, ed. J. Bryson (London, 1954) p. 571.

22. R. E. Lane, 'The Fear of Equality', *The American Political Science Review*, LIII (1959) 35ff. The author's findings bear out J. K. Galbraith's statement (*The Affluent Society* (London, 1958) ch. 7, sect. ii; pp. 76–8 of the Pelican Book edn, 1962) that few things are more evident in modern social history, particularly in the United States, than the decline in concern for inequality as an economic issue.

23. For further illustrations of this point see J. Plamenatz's 'Diversity of Rights and Kinds of Equality', in *Equality* (Nomos IX), ed. J. R. Pennock and J. W. Chapman (New York, 1967) pp. 79–83. Locke mentions a number of exceptions (of a partly moral nature) to man's natural equality in his *Second Treatise of Government*, sect. 54.

24. Hobbes, *Leviathan*, ed. W. G. Pogson Smith (Oxford, 1909; 1967 impression) chs 13, 15, pp. 94–5, 117–18.

25. For previous expositions of similar points see D. D. Raphael, 'Equality and Equity', *Philosophy*, XXI (1946) and my paper 'On Justifying Inequality', *Political Studies*, XI (1963); also R. J. Delahunty, 'The Conflict between Liberty and Equality', *Durham University Journal*, 72 (1980) 137–8.

26. With regard to this formulation my approach does not differ significantly from that put forward by S. I. Benn and R. S. Peters in their *Social Principles and the Democratic State* (London, 1959) ch. 5.

27. My formulation of the weak and strong senses of the principle of equality differs from that advanced by Brian Barry in his *Political Argument* (London, 1965) ch. VII. Like Benn's and Peters's, it may be, as he puts it (p. 120, n.1), an 'emasculation' of the concept of equality in comparison with his own. The reason for my cautiousness is that any stronger definition of equality involves difficulties, some of which have already been alluded to, while others will be dealt with at a later stage, where I discuss the concept in connection with Aristotle's criteria for differentiation on the basis of the various categories.

28. For a consideration of some of these see H. A. Bedau's opening essay 'Egalitarianism and the Idea of Equality' in *Equality* (Nomos IX), ed.

Pennock and Chapman. This is reprinted in a revised but shortened form under the title 'Radical Egalitarianism' in *Justice and Equality*, ed. H. A. Bedau (Englewood Cliffs, N.J., 1971) pp. 168–80.

29. The examples are taken from Michael Young, *The Rise of the Meritocracy* (London, 1958) p. 124.

30. A. D. Lindsay, *The Modern Democratic State* (London, 1943) pp. 260–1. For Lindsay, this kind of democratic levelling-down can be dismissed not only because of its false and abstract view of things, but also on account of the doctrine of the 'identity of indiscernibles', whose moral is that only qualitatively as well as numerically *different* things or people can be equal.

31. This point will be taken up again in ch. 3, sect. ii, penultimate para.

32. *Nic. Ethics*, Bk V, ch. iii, sect. 11, 1131 b 5–6.

33. Compare John Rawls' argument that the notions of reciprocity and contract between rational and autonomous persons are central to the principles of both fairness and justice ('Justice as Fairness', *The Philosophical Review*, LXVII (1958); reprinted in *Philosophy, Politics and Society*, ed. P. Laslett and W. G. Runciman (Oxford, 2nd series, 1962)). That there is a certain analogy between Aristotle's and Rawls's analyses is stated by Rawls himself ('Constitutional Liberty and the Concept of Justice', in *Justice* (Nomos VI), ed. C. J. Friedrich and J. W. Chapman (New York, 1963) p. 125). See also C. Fried, 'Justice and Liberty', in ibid., p. 131.

34. See above, previous paragraph.

35. *Nic. Ethics*, Bk V, ch. v, sects 6–8, 1132 b 31–1133 a 8.

36. Ibid., sect. 12, 1133 b 4–6; see ch. iii, sect. 11, 1131 b 5–6.

37. Ibid., sects 10–11, 1133 a 19–31; sects 13–16, 1133 b 6–28.

38. Compare C. Kirwan's Critical Notice on W. F. R. Hardie, *Aristotle's Ethical Theory* (Oxford, 1968) in *Mind*, 79 (1970) 450–1.

39. *Nic. Ethics*, Bk V, ch. v, sect. 9, 1133 a 16–18 (my italics).

40. Ibid., sect. 14, 1133 b 18–20 (my italics).

41. Sir Alexander Grant, *The Ethics of Aristotle* (London, 1866, 2nd edn) vol. II, p. 119, note on sect. 9.

42. Cf. *The Works of Aristotle translated into English*, ed. W. D. Ross (Oxford, 1915) vol. IX (trans. W. D. Ross), note on *Nic. Ethics*, 1133 b 3.

43. For him, occupational trades and social classes are all 'parts of the State'. See W. L. Newman's edition of Aristotle's *Politics* (Oxford, 1887–92) vol. I, p. 98.

44. *Politics*, Bk IV, ch. iv, sects 11ff.; see also sect. 21. For a more general critique of Plato's political community and the position he assigns to the farming class see Bk II, chs v and vi. For farmers and artisans in the state planned by Hippodamus, see Bk II, ch. viii, sects 2–12.

45. In his description of the ideal state (*Politics*, Bk VII, ch. x, sects 13–14), Aristotle specifies that slaves are preferable to serfs as agricultural

labourers. I shall not enter here into a discussion of his notions concerning the necessity of slavery, nor of what he has to say about the treatment and eventual emancipation of slaves.

46. *Politics*, Bk VI, ch. iv, sect. 1. Barker, in his edition (p. 263, n. 2), remarks that 'the agrarian (we may even say the anti-commercial and anti-industrial) trend of Aristotle's thought has already been expressed in the first book of the *Politics*, cc. ix–xi'.

47. Ibid., sect. 12.

48. For a fuller exposition of the superiority of spiritual over external goods and those of the body, see Aristotle's account of an ideal constitution in *Politics*, Bk VII, ch. i.

49. The three criteria mentioned in this paragraph are stated summarily and in conjunction in *Politics*, Bk IV, ch. i, sect. 10.

50. *Politics*, Bk III, ch. vi, sect. 11. In sect. 9, Aristotle squares the standard of absolute justice with 'the natural system', especially that followed in more ancient times, when men believed that they ought to rule in turns, and that whenever anyone was in office he would serve the interest of those who were not. See below, ch. 4, sect. iii, para. 5, and sect. vi, para. 4 from the end.

51. *Politics*, Bk IV, ch. i, sects 9–11.

52. Though accidental, number remains for Aristotle a characteristic or attribute of the two constitutions under discussion, since it normally happens that only a few in a state are rich and the poor are numerous.

53. *Politics*, Bk III, ch. viii; Bk IV, ch. iv.

54. Sir John A. R. Marriott, *English Political Institutions* (Oxford, 1938, 4th edn) p. 11.

55. Indeed, the numerical criterion has survived as the more prominent and instructive factor in modern classifications of constitutions. Marriott's own division consists of the following three kinds: (a) simple (unitary) or composite (federal); (b) rigid or flexible; (c) monarchical (presidential) or parliamentary.

56. Cf. here Newman's edition of the *Politics*, vol. I, pp. 214–25.

57. See p. 256, n. 1 in Barker's edition of the *Politics*.

58. *Politics*, Bk III, ch. iv.

59. Ibid., sect. 6.

60. Cf. ibid., Bk III, ch. iv; Bk I, ch. xiii; and above all the *locus classicus* on the subject, *Nic. Ethics*, Bk I, ch. vi, 1096 a 19ff., where (as in *Eudemian Ethics*, Bk I, ch. viii, 1217 b 25–41) Aristotle explains that, though the word 'good' (along with other 'syncategorematic' words like 'unity' or 'being') can be applied in all the categories, its meaning nevertheless varies with each.

61. *Politics*, Bk III, ch. v. For the same distinction in the structure of an 'ideal state' see Bk VII, ch. viii.

62. *Politics*, Bk IV, ch. iii, sect. 5.

63. *Politics*, Bk VI, ch. i, sect. 8.

64. *Politics*, Bk IV, ch. vi.
65. See also *Politics*, Bk IV, ch. xii, sect. 3. That the order of priority is both logical and temporal is clear from Bk IV, ch. vi, sects 3 and 5, and from Bk VI, ch. iv, sect. 1.
66. The disadvantages of poverty were compensated for by payment for attendance in the assembly and the courts.
67. See also *Politics*, Bk IV, ch. xv, sects 12–13; Bk VI, ch. ii, sects 6–7; ch. v, sects 5ff.; Bk VII, ch. iv; and Bk IV, ch. xiii, sect. 5.
68. For a full account, see Newman's edition of the *Politics*, vol. IV, pp. xxxvi–lxi. The reasons for the differences of esteem accorded to farmers, artisans, traders, etc., are explained in vol. I, pp. 98–139.
69. *Politics*, Bk VI, ch. iv, sects 15–20; ch. v, sect. 5; Bk V, ch. v.
70. *Politics*, Bk III, ch. x, sect. 1.
71. Ibid., ch. xiii, sects 4–5.
72. See Barker's footnote on p. 121 of his edition of the *Politics*.
73. J. S. Mill, too, speaks of two conflicting influences in all human affairs, yet each with its own quite definite advantages and such as 'to keep one another alive and efficient'. What he has in mind are a representative democracy on the one hand, and government in the hands of professional administrators on the other *(Representative Government*, ed. R. B. McCallum, ch. VI, pp. 178–81 (Oxford, 1946)). See also *On Liberty*, ch. V, pp. 99–104, and particularly Mill's compromise solution to this issue, i.e. 'the greatest dissemination of power consistent with efficiency' (p. 102).
74. The relevant passages are in the *Politics*, Bk III, chs x–xi, xiii, xv–xvi.
75. For this phrase see J. S. Mill, *Representative Government*, ch. VI, p. 178.
76. *Politics*, Bk III, ch. xi. Compare Mill's statement that what can be done better by a popular assembly than by any individual is deliberation *(Representative Government*, ch. V, p. 164).
77. *Politics*, Bk III, ch. xi, sects 2, 9, 14. Compare here Rousseau's similar arguments (in the context of his doctrine of the General Will) that, when assembled, the people may judge soundly, though individually their judgement is imperfect *(The Social Contract*, Bk II, ch. iii; ch. iv, para. 7; ch. vi, last para.). See also his *Discourse on Political Economy* (p. 238, Everyman edn), where the principle that the voice of the people is the voice of God is vindicated. As G. C. Lichtenberg remarked: 'In the words: *Vox populi vox Dei* lies more wisdom than is currently found in any other four words' *(Werke*, ed. R. K. Goldschmit (Stuttgart, 1924) p. 221; my trans.).
78. For the significance of the 'Shoe Pinching' argument and other such claims for the democratic control of government see A. D. Lindsay, *The Modern Democratic State*, pp. 267–86.
79. *Politics*, Bk III, ch. xi, sect. 14.
80. Ibid., ch. xv, sects 8–9; ch. xvi, sects 3–5, 8–9, 11.

81. G. Le Bon, *The Crowd* (London, 1896); W. Trotter, *Instincts of the Herd in Peace and War* (London, 1916).
82. In the present context there is no need to distinguish between the two.
83. For Rousseau's scruples in this connection see his *Discourse on the Origin of Inequality*, Dedication (1762; Everyman edn, London, 1946) pp. 146–7.
84. That a *koinōnia* arises only between those who are different is explicitly stated (as we have seen earlier) in *Nic. Ethics*, Bk V, ch. v, sect. 9, 1133 a 16ff. For differentiation as one of the main characteristics of political life see Newman's edition of the *Politics*, vol. I, pp. 90–8.

Notes to Chapter 2: Two Definitions of Equality

1. *Physics*, Bk VII, ch. iv.
2. For the different senses of 'one', see also *Metaphysics*, Δ, ch. vi; I, ch. i. Both for the sake of convention and in order to avoid ambiguity, Greek capitals are used for the numbering of the books of Aristotle's *Metaphysics*.
3. See also *Metaphysics*, Δ, ch. xv, 1021 a 6–7.
4. Russell, *The Principles of Mathematics* (London, 1903; 2nd edn, 1937) p. 159.
5. See ibid., pp. 167–8, 218–19; F. Waismann, *Introduction to Mathematical Thinking* (London, 1951) pp. 29ff. and 55–6.
6. The word 'quality' could, of course, be so applied, but then (a) this word is not specifically descriptive as 'sweet' or 'sharp' is, and (b) its use in connection with warmness, sweetness and whiteness could be taken to indicate that these three qualities differ in kind rather than that the word 'quality' is itself ambiguous; if applied to softness and hardness, on the other hand, 'quality' could be taken to indicate that there is a difference of degree between these two properties.
7. This parlance, however, appears legitimate if differences of brightness, shade or saturation (as opposed to hue) between the different species of colour are to be expressed.
8. See also *Categories*, ch. vi, 6 a 26–35.
9. *Metaphysics*, Λ, ch. iv, 1070 b 7 (ta *noēta*). The topic I am about to discuss as part of Aristotle's doctrine may also be raised in connection with Plato's, particularly in the *Parmenides*. I shall not mention Plato here (particularly as Gilbert Ryle has done this so fully in his two 'Parmenides' articles in *Mind* for April and July 1939), and instead concentrate on points often stated by Aristotle more explicitly than by Plato. The analogy formulated in this paragraph between *koinōnia* and *ta koina* will be qualified subsequently.
10. *Metaphysics*, Γ, ch. ii, 1003 b 35–6.
11. Some of these terms also occur in *Met.*, B, ch. i, 995 b 20–5, and in Δ, chs vi, vii, ix–xi, xv–vi, xxv–vi, xxviii.

12. *Met.*, Δ, ch. xv, 1021 a.
13. *Posterior Analytics*, Bk I, ch. x, 76 b 10–11; *Met.*, B, ch.ii, 996 b 28–30. Similarly in *Topics*, Bk IV, ch. i, 121 b 7, and ch. vi, 127 a 27–8.
14. *Post. Anal.*, Bk I, ch. x, 76 a 38–42, 76 b 12–21; *Met.*, K, ch.iv, 1061 b 18–21.
15. Or have 'communion' with one another in virtue of the common notions (*epikoinōnousi kata ta koina*) (ibid., ch. xi, 77 a 26–7).
16. For a different interpretation of Aristotle's concept of good, which does not assimilate it to the 'transcategorial' notion of being or unity, see J. L. Ackrill, 'Aristotle on "Good" and the Categories', in *Articles on Aristotle: 2. Ethics and Politics*, ed. J. Barnes, M. Schofield and R. Sorabji (London, 1977) pp. 17–24; also in *Islamic Philosophy and the Classical Tradition*, ed. Stern (Oxford, 1973).
17. Gilbert Ryle, *Dilemmas* (Cambridge, 1954) pp. 115ff. In a letter to me, dated 24 December 1960, Ryle writes: 'Aristotle has a doctrine of "Koina" – "common" terms – where "common" at least means "bound to be present in discourse on any topic whatsoever", and so not proprietary to astronomy or medicine or politics etc.' In *Plato's Progress* (Cambridge, 1966), Ryle refers to common notions and common truths as 'ubiquitous', 'non-specialist' or 'transdepartmental', that is as 'neutral between all the departments of thought and knowledge' (pp. 132–5, 276–7, 292–3).
18. J. L. Austin, *Sense and Sensibilia* (Oxford, 1962) pp. 64–71.
19. R. G. Collingwood, *An Essay on Philosophical Method* (Oxford, 1933) pp. 32–3.
20. G. E. L. Owen has confirmed to me that in the context under discussion the translation of *to einai* as 'exist' (rather than as 'to be') is legitimate. For the point generally see his 'Notes on Ryle's Plato', in *Ryle*, ed. O. P. Wood and G. Pitcher (London, 1971) p. 343.
21. *Met.*, Z, ch. xiii, 1038 b 8–12; ch. xvi, 1040 b 16–26; I, ch. ii, 1053 b 16–21. For a more detailed analysis and further references to the topics in Aristotle's writings dealt with here see my 'Existence: a Humean Point in Aristotle's Metaphysics', *The Review of Metaphysics,* XIII (1960) 597–604.
22. What holds good for 'unity' holds good for numerical terms in general. 'You would know *nothing* as to the topic of a conversation if you merely heard number-words occurring in it from time to time' (G. E. M. Anscombe and P. T. Geach, *Three Philosophers* (Oxford, 1961) pp. 73–4).
23. *Met.*, A, 992 b 18ff.; Γ, 1003 a 33–b 36; Δ, ch. vii; E, 1026 a 33ff.; Z, ch. i; H, 1042 b 25ff.; I, 1054 a 13–19. Also compare Franz Brentano, *On the Several Senses of Being in Aristotle*, ed. and trans. by Rolf George (Berkeley and London, 1975).
24. Gilbert Ryle, *Philosophical Arguments*, an Inaugural Lecture (Oxford, 1945) p. 16.

25. Letter of 24 December 1960. Here he is alluding to my article in the *Review of Metaphysics*, referred to above. The italics are Ryle's.
26. *Met.* Γ, ch. ii.
27. Ibid., ch. iii, 1005 a 19–29. For axioms as *common* principles (*koina*) see *Post. Anal.,* Bk I, ch. x, 76 a 38–42, 76 b 14; ch. xi, 77 a 27–9; ch. xxxii, 88 a 36–b 8.
28. *Met.*, B, 996 b 28.
29. Though to say 'he is equally good at playing football and the flute' would involve something of a category confusion.
30. *Met.*, Γ, ch. ii, 1004 a 1–2; also 9–10, 17–20.
31. There is a 'Selection of Contraries' in Fr. 1478 b 36–1479 a 5 (Fr. 31 in *Fragmenta*, ed. V. Rose (Leipzig, 1886)).
32. The statement concerning the deducibility of all pairs of opposites from unity and plurality already occurs in *Met.*, Γ, ch. ii, 1004 a 19, and Δ, ch. xv, 1021 a 9–11.
33. *Met.*, Γ, ch. ii, 1004 a 22–3. One set of meanings of the word 'one' (i.e. the continuous, the whole, the individual and the universal) is specified in I, ch. i; another in Δ, ch. vi.
34. *Met.*, Δ1017 a 22–7; I, 1053 b 24–5, 1054 a 13–15.
35. For example, *Met.*, Δ, 1021 a 8–12. See the Appendix.
36. *Met.*, Δ, 1021 a 6–14.
37. *Met.*, I, 1052 b 22.
38. *Met.*, Δ, ch. xiii.
39. *Met.*, Γ, 1004 a 17–23.
40. *Met.*, Δ, 1024 b 9–15; I, 1054 b 23–1055 a 10; also Δ, 1018 a 9–15.

Notes to Chapter 3: Justifiable Inequality and Civic Excellence

1. *Politics*, Bk I, ch. i, sect. 1, 1252 a 1.
2. *Politics*, Bk II, ch. ix, sect. 22, and Barker's notes (pp. 80, 234) containing further references to Aristotle's idea that will is the basis of the state.
3. *Politics*, Bk III, ch. vi, sects 2–5. Compare *Nic. Ethics*, Bk IX, ch. vi, sect. 1: 'states are said to be unanimous when their members have the same conception of their interest; will the same objects; and execute common resolves'.
4. *Nic. Ethics*, Bk VIII, ch. ix, sect. 1, 1159 b 25–7; 1160 a 9–23. For an analysis of Aristotle's definition of the meaning of *koinōnia* see Newman's edition of the *Politics*, vol. I, pp. 41–4.
5. See ch. 1, sect. iii, penultimate para.
6. *Politics*, Bk VII, ch. iii, sect. 9, 1325 b 26–7.
7. Ibid., ch. viii, sects 1–2, 1328 a 21–6.
8. Cf. also *Politics*, Bk III, ch. i, sect. 2, 1274 b 38–40.
9. *Politics*, Bk I, ch. v, sect. 3, 1254 a 28–31.
10. *Nic. Ethics*, Bk IX, ch. viii, sect. 6, 1168 b 31–2. See also Barker's

note appended to the passage from the *Politics*, Bk III, ch. i, sect. 2 (cited above), pp. 95–6.

11. *Politics*, Bk VII, ch. viii, sect. 2, 1328 a 25–6.
12. *Metaphysics*, △, 1016 a 24–7. See Newman's edition of the *Politics*, vol. I, p. 43, n. 1.
13. See above, ch. 2, sect. i.
14. *Politics*, Bk VII, ch. viii, sect. 4, 1328 a 35–6.
15. Newman, vol. III, p. 374, note on 1328 a 36.
16. *Politics*, Bk VII, ch. viii, sect. 2, 1328 a 25–7.
17. Ibid., sect. 4, 1328 a 36–7. In Bk V, ch. viii, sects 5–7. Aristotle has more to say about the 'democratic spirit of equality' in the context of his inquiry into the methods of ensuring constitutional stability. He points to the fact that some states owe their stability to the good relations which their officers have with the rest of the citizens, including the masses and the unenfranchised. Subsequently, however, he advocates that the principle of equality should in all justice extend only to those who are really 'peers'. This view he follows up with the remark that expediency is as important as what is just, and that in the presence of a policy (such as the one advocated), family cliques are less likely to gain the upper hand in a state. On the other hand, he observes, there is the risk of demagogues emerging in a numerous class of 'peers'. In this way Aristotle passes from a matter of high principle to considerations of utility and risk – all within the ambit of the principle of equality.
18. Ibid., 1328 a 38–40.
19. Ibid., 1328 a 40–b 2 (my italics); similarly in Bk III, 1275 a 35–1275 b 5.
20. *Politics*, Bk III, ch. iv, sect. 6, 1277 a 5; also 1276 b 28, 40.
21. *Politics*, Bk II, ch. ii, sect. 3, 1261 a 22–4 (italics in Barker's edition, p. 41); compare 1261 a 29–30: 'for a city to be a real unity it must be made up of elements which *differ in kind*' (my italics).
22. *Politics*, Bk II, ch. i, sect. 1, 1260 b 27–8, 40.
23. As explained above (ch. 1, sect. iii), Aristotle makes the same point in his *Nic. Ethics*, Bk V, ch. v, sect. 6, 1132 b 31–4: 'But in associations for exchange such a sort of justice as reciprocation forms the bond of union – reciprocity according to proportion and not exact equality. For it is by proportionate reciprocity of action that the social community is held together.' He adds in ch. vi, sects 3–4, 1134 a 24–8, that the relation between the principle of reciprocity and political justice is found among men who share their life with a view to self-sufficiency and who are free and equal, either proportionally (as for Aristotle) or numerically (as in a democracy).
24. Newman, vol. II, pp. 233–4, note on 1261 a 30ff.
25. I am summarising here the contents of the *Politics*, Bk II, ch. ii, sects 4–7.
26. *Politics*, Bk IV, ch. xi, sect. 8, 1295 b 25–6.

27. Cf. *Politics*, Bk III, ch. vi, sects 9, 11, 1279 a 9–10, 21, where a state with the 'right' constitution is referred to as an 'association of equals and freemen'.
28. As Newman (vol. IV, p. 214, note on 1295 b 24–5) explains, 'the general inclination of foes to give each other a wide berth'.
29. See Newman's note (ibid., 1295 b 25). See also *Eud. Ethics*, Bk VII, ch. x, 1242 b 30: 'Civic friendship, then, *claims* to be resting on equality' (my italics).
30. *Politics*, Bk III, ch. iv, sect. 6, 1277 a 5.
31. Cf. *Politics*, Bk I, ch. vii, sect. 1, 1255 b 16–20. See also Bk III, ch. iv, sects 11–15, and ch. vi, sects 5–9 (particularly 1279 a 8–10). For a similar contrast in Locke see *The Second Treatise of Government*, sects 2, 23, 85, 163; for the contrast in St Thomas Aquinas and Rousseau, compare my *Hobbes and Locke: The Politics of Freedom and Obligation* (London & New York, 1982) pp. 147–8.
32. *Politics*, Bk III, ch. i, sect. 2.
33. *Politics*, Bk I, ch. v, sect. 3.
34. *Politics*, Bk IV, ch. iv, sects 9–19. See above, ch. 1, sect. iv, para. 2.
35. Barker, *The Politics of Aristotle* (Oxford, 1946) p. 160, n. 2.
36. *Politics*, Bk VII, ch. viii, sect. 1; ch. ix, sect. 10.
37. See *Politics*, Bk I, ch. ii, sect. 8.
38. *Politics*, Bk III, ch. ix, 1280 b 40–1281 a 2.
39. See my previous analysis of *Politics*, Bk II, ch. ii, in ch. 3, sect. i, paras 8 foll.
40. *Politics*, Bk IV, ch. xii, sect. 1: Bk III, ch. xii, sects 8–9; ch. xiii; and *passim*, particularly with reference to the character of oligarchies (see Bk IV, ch. iv, sect. 22; Bk VI, ch. ii, sect. 7).
41. *Politics*, Bk IV, ch. xii, sects 2–4.
42. *Politics*, Bk III, ch. xii.
43. For Plato's defence of plutocracy see his *Laws*, Bk V, 744 Bff., and K. R. Popper, *The Open Society and its Enemies* (London, 1962) vol. I, ch. 6, p. 256, n. 20.
44. *Politics*, Bk III, ch. xii, sects 8–9.
45. Ibid., ch. xiii.
46. *Paideia*, i.e. general education.
47. I follow here Newman's exegesis (vol. III, pp. 235–6, note on 1283 a 37–40).
48. The competing claims on behalf of the sovereignty of the people and the ideals of democratic equality on the one hand, and the superiority of experts or the few better citizens on the other, are assessed by Aristotle in the *Politics*, Bk III, chs x, xi, xv, in addition to ch. xiii, presently under review. For details, see above, ch. 1, sect. iv.
49. *Politics*, Bk III, ch. xiii, 1283 b 40–1.
50. Ibid., sect. 13.
51. Ibid., sect. 22.

52. Ibid., sects 13–15.
53. Ibid., sects 24–5.
54. For the use of this term in this context see *Politics*, Bk III, ch. xvii, sects 6, 7.
55. Barker's note to this effect (*The Politics of Aristotle*, p. 151, n. 2) seems to be most apposite.
56. *Politics*, Bk V, chs viii–ix.
57. Ibid., ch. viii.
58. Ibid., ch. ix.
59. Newman, vol. IV, p. 404, note on 1309 b 3–4.
60. *Politics*, Bk III, ch. xvii, sect. 4 (my italics). For an interpretation see Barker's note GG in *The Politics of Aristotle*, p. 151. Newman is silent on this point.
61. For further discussion see D. D. Raphael, 'Equality and Equity', *Philosophy*, XXI (1946); my paper 'On Justifying Inequality', *Political Studies*, XI (1963) 64ff.; and R. E. Ewin, 'On Justice and Injustice', *Mind*, LXXIX (1970) 207–8.
62. *Politics*, Bk III, ch. iv, sect. 14.
63. *Politics*, Bk VII, ch. ix, sect. 5.
64. Ibid., ch. ii, sect. 17.
65. *Politics*, Bk VII, chs viii–ix.
66. *Politics*, Bk IV, ch. iv; also Bk III, ch. ix.
67. Ibid., sect. 22; also Bk IV, ch. iii, sect. 4, and Bk VI, ch. ii, sect. 7.
68. Ideological and other contextual criteria of necessity influence any grading of social merit. Marxism extols the status of the working man and the commissar, whereas capitalism values the technocrat and the tycoon. Prussian élitism from the 18th century onwards singled out the military class and the civil servant, while in England, besides the aristocracy, the squire and the vicar represented favoured classes. While a university professor in Germany finds himself near the top of the social ladder, in America he is placed not far from the middle and certainly lower than a medical practitioner.
69. See here J. L. Evans, 'Grade not', *Philosophy*, XXXVII (1962) 30ff. Also above, ch. 1, sect. iii, para. 7.
70. *Politics*, Bk IV, ch. iii, sect. 5, 1290 a 7–10.
71. For Newman's views, see vol. I, Appendix A, pp. 565–6; vol. IV, pp. 155–6, note on 1290 a 7–10. For the variants of the text see W. D. Ross (ed.), *Aristotelis Politica* (Oxford, 1957) p. 113.
72. This is the sense given to the phrase in Richard Robinson's translation (*Aristotle's Politics, Books III and IV*, translated with Introduction and Comments (Oxford, 1962) p. 74).
73. See also *Politics*, Bk III, ch. xvi, sects 2–4; ch. xvii, sect. 2; Bk IV, ch. xi, sect. 8; and Bk VII, ch. viii, sect. 4, and the different contexts in which this phrase occurs there.
74. *Politics*, Bk IV, ch. xi, sects 7–8.

75. Newman, vol. IV, p. 215, note on 1295 b 27–8.
76. My italics.
77. *Politics*, Bk VI, ch. ii.
78. For example, *Politics*, Bk III, ch. x, sects 1–3; Bk VI, ch. iii, sect. 3.
79. For example, *Politics*, Bk V, ch. ix, sects 15–16; ch. xii, sect. 18; Bk VI, ch. iv, sect. 20.
80. This is Barker's conjecture (p. 259, n. 5), and I accept it as plausible. Newman, too, is inclined to interpret the passage in this way, and his cross-reference, like Barker's, is to *Politics*, Bk IV, ch. iv, sects 22–4, 1291 b 30–8 (Newman, vol. IV, p. 504, note on 1318 a 5–6). Sir David Ross, too, has a cross-reference to 1291 b 32 (*Aristotelis Politica*, p.194, note on 1318 a 7).
81. Barker's translation shows this clearly, whereas the Everyman translation overlooks this finesse and, in addition, is not free from error.
82. My italics.
83. The idea of representation is also referred to by Aristotle in *Politics*, Bk IV, ch. xiv, sect. 13, where he stipulates that the parts of a democratic state should be represented in the assembly by an equal number of members, either elected or appointed by lot. I should add here that the criteria of assessment for the calculus – amount of property and number of property owners – are anticipated in *Politics*, Bk III, 1282 a 29–41.
84. As Newman (vol. iv, p. 507, note on 1318 b 1–3) points out with examples, there is an allusion here to a common saying in antiquity.
85. *Politics*, Bk VI, ch. iii, sect. 6, 1318 b 4–5.
86. *Politics*, Bk V, ch. ii, sect. 3, 1302 a 29–31; Bk II, ch. vii, sect. 10, 1266 b 40–1267 a 1.

Notes to Chapter 4: Revolution and the Law

1. For a student revolutionary's views on the matter see the description by Brian MacArthur in the third article of the series 'The Revolutionaries' in *The Times* of 17 February 1971, p. 14: 'He would describe himself as a revolutionary, he says, only in the sense that many of his aims, such as social justice, equality of opportunity, an end to poverty, and decent housing, could not be brought about short of revolution, since parliamentary democracy offers no effective choice whatsoever.'
2. *Politics*, Bk V, ch. vii, sects 11–12; see Bk V, ch. iii, sect. 10; ch. iv, sects 1–7.
3. Ibid., ch. viii, sect. 6.
4. Ibid., ch. vi, sect. 6; also ch. v.
5. Newman, vol. IV, p. 352, note on 1305 b 30.
6. *Politics*, Bk V, ch. v, sect. 10, 1305 a 29–32; Bk IV, ch. iv, sect. 29.
7. *Politics*, Bk V, ch. viii, sects 13–14.

8. *Politics*, Bk II, ch. vii, sect. 10.
9. *Politics*, Bk IV, ch. xi, sects 16–17; also sect. 13.
10. *Politics*, Bk IV, ch. xi, sects 8, 10, 12–15; ch. xii, sects 4–6; Bk V, ch. vii, sects 5–8.
11. Ibid., ch. ix, sects 6–8; see also Bk IV, chs ix-xi.
12. *Politics*, Bk III, ch. xii, sects 1–2; also ch. ix, sect. 1.
13. *Politics*, Bk V, ch. iii, sect. 14, 1303 b 3–7. The placing of this section is in doubt. Newman suggests that it should be inserted at the end of ch. 1, sect. 5, 1301 a 39 (Newman, vol. IV, p. 316, note on 1303 b 3; also p. 33, n. 1). Sir David Ross takes note of this suggestion, though without effecting the transposition (*Aristotelis Politica*, p. 152, note on 1303 b 3).
14. *Politics*, Bk V, ch. ii, sect. 3, 1302 a 28–9.
15. See above, ch. 3, sect. iii, paragraph towards the end, beginning: 'Aristotle draws a number . . .'
16. Compare Wittgenstein's comment (1 January 1931) on Soviet Russia: 'Die Leidenschaft verspricht etwas. Unser Gerede dagegen is kraftlos.' (In F. Waismann, *Wittgenstein und der Wiener Kreis*, ed. B. F. McGuinness (Oxford, 1967) p. 142; English translation by J. Schulte and McGuinness (Oxford, 1979).)
17. For example *Politics*, Bk IV, ch. xi, sects 1–3; Bk VII, ch. i, sects 1ff.
18. For an application of such a Wittgensteinian approach to social and political theory and particularly to the systematic ambiguity arising in controversies in this context see Hanna F. Pitkin, *Wittgenstein and Justice* (Berkeley, 1972) especially ch. viii.
19. *Politics*, Bk III, ch. ix, , sects 1–4; ch. xiii.
20. Ibid., sect. 9.
21. Ibid., sects 14, 21–3.
22. *Nic. Ethics*, Bk V, ch. vii, sect. 4, 1134 b 33–5.
23. *Politics*, Bk I, chs i, ii. See also D. J. Allan, *The Philosophy of Aristotle* (London, 1952) pp. 32–5, and R. G. Collingwood, *The Idea of Nature* (Oxford, 1945) pp. 80–2.
24. For useful critical comments on Aristotle's views on the proper ends of a state and the purposes of political life in general see Richard Robinson, *Aristotle's Politics, Books III and IV*, Introduction, sects 6 and 7.
25. *Politics*, Bk I, ch. ii, sect. 15.
26. See Barker's Introduction to the *Politics*, pp. xlix–l.
27. *Nic. Ethics*, Bk V, ch. vii, sect. 2, 1134 b 24–7. See below, ch. 4, sect. v, para. 8.
28. The distinction has been discussed frequently in modern times. For an early account see Karl Pearson's *The Grammar of Science* (London, 1892) ch. III, especially sect. 5.
29. For further details see S. I. Benn and R. S. Peters, *Social Principles and the Democratic State* (London, 1959) pp. 15–18; H. L. A. Hart,

The Concept of Law (Oxford, 1961) pp. 182–3; K. R. Popper, *The Open Society and its Enemies* (London, 1945) vol. I, ch. 5: 'Nature and Convention'.

30. *Nic. Ethics*, Bk V, ch. vii, sect. 5, 1134 b 35–1135 a 5.
31. Ibid., sect. 1, 1134 b 18–24.
32. Ibid., ch. v, sects 10–16, 1133 a 19–b 28. For Locke's views on the conventional basis of money and its use, see his *Second Treatise of Government*, sects 36–50.
33. See above, ch. 1, sect. iii, second half.
34. Discussed above, ch. 1, sect. iii, first half. The example of the shoe, in its use both for exchange and for wearing, turns up in *Politics*, Bk I, ch. ix, sects 2–3. Reference to the shoemaker, farmer and carpenter occurs in Bk III, ch. ix, sect. 10.
35. Gilbert Ryle, *Dilemmas* (Cambridge, 1954) p. 120.
36. *Politics*, Bk I, chs viii–xi; Bk III, ch. ix; Bk VII, chs iv–vii (in the ideal state). The parallelism between the two conventional institutions of money and language, together with their effect on progress and further, more complex forms of evolution, was pointed out by Gibbon in his *History of the Decline and Fall of the Roman Empire* (London, 1900) vol. I, ch. ix, p. 220.
37. *Politics*, Bk IV, ch. i, sect. 9, and sects 10 and 11.
38. *Politics*, Bk III, ch. xvi, sects 1–4.
39. Ibid., ch. vi, sect. 9. See above, ch. 1, n. 50, and ch. 3, sect. iii, paras 7 and 8.
40. See above, ch. 4, sect. ii, para. 8.
41. See below, ch. 4, sect. vi, paras 15ff.
42. *Politics*, Bk III, ch. xvi, sect. 3. See also Bk III, ch. xvii, sect. 2; and Bk VII, ch. xiv, sects 3, 5. I may mention that R. G. Collingwood's 'Three Laws of Politics' (*The New Leviathan* (Oxford, 1943) ch. xxv) should be seen against the background of this sort of Aristotelian doctrine.
43. *Nic. Ethics*, Bk V, ch. vi, sect. 5, 1134 a 35–b 2.
44. *Politics*, Bk IV, ch. iv, sects 22–3.
45. I am following here Newman's reading of the text (Newman, vol. IV, pp. 175–6, note on 1291 b 32); see also *Politics*, Bk VI, ch. ii, sect. 9.
46. *Politics*, Bk VI, ch. iv, sects 5–10.
47. Ibid., sects 15–20.
48. *Politics*, Bk IV, ch. iv, sects 25–31.
49. *Politics*, Bk III, ch. ix, sect. 8.
50. *Politics*, Bk VI, ch. v, sects 1–4.
51. This proposition is treated by Aristotle almost as an axiom: see *Politics*, Bk V, ch. viii, sect. 1, where he states in nearly Hobbesian fashion: 'to know the causes which destroy constitutions is also to know the causes which ensure their preservation. Opposite effects are brought about by opposite causes; and destruction and preservation are opposite effects.'

52. *Politics*, Bk v, ch. vii, sects 11–14.
53. Ibid., ch. viii, sects 2, 9; ch. vii, sect. 14.
54. John Locke, *The Second Treatise of Government*, ch. xix, sects 211–21.
55. *Politics*, Bk v, ch. viii, sects 15–21.
56. *Politics*, Bk iv, ch. xii, sects 4–6; Bk v, ch. vii, sects 6–7.
57. Ibid., ch. xi, sect. 17.
58. Ibid., sect. 15.
59. *Politics*, Bk ii, ch. vii.
60. Ibid., sect. 2, 1266 a 37–8; sect. 5, 1266 b 9–10. For Locke's notion of the 'regulation' of property in civil society see *The Second Treatise of Government*, ed. P. Laslett (Cambridge, amended 2nd edn, 1970) sect. 3, line 3; sect. 45, line 10; sect. 50, line 15; sect. 120, lines 7–8.
61. *Politics*, Bk ii, ch. vii, sect. 5.
62. Ibid., sects 5–9.
63. Ibid., sects 19–20.
64. Ibid., sects 8–9.
65. Compare Rousseau, *The Social Contract* (Everyman edn, London, 1946) Bk ii, ch. xi, p. 42, para. 2.
66. See *Politics*, Bk v, ch. ix, sects 5–16.
67. Ibid., sect. 12, 1310 a 14–17.
68. *Politics*, Bk viii, ch. i, sects 2–4.
69. Rousseau, *A Discourse on the Origin of Inequality* (1762; Everyman edn, London, 1946) p. 160.
70. Rousseau, *The Social Contract* (Everyman edn) Bk i, ch. ix, p. 19, and note 1, my italics. For equality as one of the ends 'of every system of legislation', see Bk ii, ch. xi, p. 42, para. 1.
71. *Rhetoric*, Bk i, ch. xiii, sects 1–2, and ch. xv, sects 3–8 (1373b and 1375a). For an informative analysis of Aristotle's conception of law, particularly his account of the varieties of law and the extent to which he might be considered a natural-law theorist *in embryo* (together with references to the relevant literature), see D. N. Schroeder, 'Aristotle on Law', *Polis*, iv (1981) 17–31. However, while Schroeder concludes that Aristotle was neither an early exponent of natural-law doctrine nor a legal positivist, my argument in previous and subsequent sections is that Aristotle consistently and effectively combined the idea of the conventional character of positive law with that of a moral law of nature.
72. Cf. J. S. Mill, *A System of Logic* (London, 4th edn, 1866) Bk vi, ch. xi, sect. 2 (vol. ii, pp. 520–1); also P. H. Nowell-Smith, *Ethics* (London, 1954) pp. 236–9.
73. Cf. J. D. Mabbott, 'Punishment', *Mind*, xlviii (1939) (reprinted in *The Philosophy of Punishment*, ed. H. B. Acton (London, 1969) ch. 2).
74. In S. E. Toulmin's and John Rawls' sense of the word: see Toulmin, *The Place of Reason in Ethics* (Cambridge, 1950) pp. 150ff.; and

Rawls, 'Two Concepts of Rules', *The Philosophical Review*, LXIV (1955) (reprinted in *Theories of Ethics*, ed. P. Foot (London, 1967) ch. xi). For the point of difference involved in this passage, see *Nic. Ethics*, Bk V, ch. vii, 1135 a 5–12.

75. See R. E. Ewin, 'On Justice and Injustice', *Mind*, LXXIX (1970). For the argument that, *pace* Lon Fuller's endeavour (*The Morality of Law* (New Haven, 1964)) to vindicate traditional natural-law theory, no moral standards are intrinsic to the concept of law nor in fact implicit in its application, see D. Lyons, 'The Internal Morality of Law', *Arist. Soc. Proc.,* LXXI (1970–1).

76. *Politics*, Bk IV, ch. viii, sect. 6.

77. Ibid., ch. i, sect. 9.

78. See John Rawls, 'Justice as Fairness', *The Philosophical Review*, LXVII (1958) (reprinted in *Philosophy, Politics and Society*, ed. P. Laslett and W. G. Runciman, 2nd series (Oxford, 2nd series, 1962) ch. 7); see also his 'Distributive Justice', in ibid. (Oxford, 3rd series, 1967) ch. 3.

79. *Politics*, Bk I, ch. i, sect. 1, 1252 a 1. For a reference to experience, as a result of which existing laws may be improved see Bk III, ch. xvi, sect. 5.

80. Ibid. In his reference to the traditional doctrine of a divine natural law (*The Social Contract*, Bk II, ch. vi, paras 2–3), Rousseau likewise states that universal justice 'comes from God ... emanating from reason alone'.

81. *Nic. Ethics*, Bk I, ch. vii, particularly 1098 a 1–14.

82. Ibid., 1098 b 2–4.

83. See my edition of Locke's *Essays on the Law of Nature* (Oxford, 1954) p. 112.

84. Bishop Butler, *The Analogy of Religion* (London, 1736) pt I, ch. i, sect. 31 (*Works*, ed. W. E. Gladstone (Oxford, 1896) vol. I, p. 46).

85. *Rhetoric*, Bk I, ch. xiii, sect. 2, and ch. xv, sect. 6.

86. See John Yolton, *John Locke and the Way of Ideas* (London, 1956) pp. 26–48; D. J. O'Connor, *Aquinas and Natural Law* (London, 1967) pp. 41–4, 61.

87. For the importance of Aristotle's *indirect* influence upon the notion of natural law see P. M. Farrell, 'Sources of St Thomas' Concept of Natural Law', *The Thomist*, XX (1957) 254.

88. *Politics*, Bk VII, ch. xiii, sects 10–13; also ch. xv, sects 7–10. Compare B. Jowett's *The Politics of Aristotle* (Oxford, 1885) vol. II, pt i, p. 281, on 13.11.

89. *Politics*, Bk II, ch. v, sects 8–10; *Nic. Ethics*, Bk IX, ch. viii; Newman, vol. II, pp. 251ff.; Grant, *The Ethics of Aristotle* (London, 1866, 2nd edn) vol. II, pp. 297, 300 (notes), particularly for a comparison between Aristotle's and Bishop Butler's description of self-love. For an assessment of the roles of natural virtue and self-love in Aristotle's ethics, see W. F. R. Hardie, *Aristotle's Ethical Theory* (Oxford, 1968) pp. 176–80, 323–35.

90. *Nic. Ethics*, Bk VI, ch. xiii; Bk VII, ch. viii, 1151 a 18; Bk X, ch. ix, 1179 b 20–1180 a 5; *Eud. Ethics*, Bk III, ch. vii, 1234 a 28. For the *Magna Moralia* see Bk I, ch. xxxiv, 1197 b 36–1198 a 9. Aristotle's statements about natural virtue are among passages examined by Anthony Kenny in his study of the three books common to the *Nicomachean* and *Eudemian Ethics* and for his reappraisal of the significance of the *Eudemian Ethics* in this as well as other contexts (*The Aristotelian Ethics* (Oxford, 1978) pp. 25, 57, 184, and particularly 188–9).

91. This passage in *Nic. Ethics*, Bk X, ch. ix, sect. 6, 1179 b 21–3, is consistent with Bk II, ch. i, sects 2–3, 1103 a 18–25, where Aristotle explains 'that none of the moral virtues arises in us by nature, but rather that we are adapted by nature to receive them, and are made perfect by habit'.

92. For the difference between *kata ton orthon logon* and *meta tou orthou logou* see *Nic. Ethics*, ed. Grant, *op.cit.*, vol II, pp. 187–8, note; J. Burnet (ed.), *The Ethics of Aristotle* (London, 1900) p. 286, notes.

93. St Thomas Aquinas, *Summa Theol.*, IaIIae, q. 94, art. i, *ad* 2 *um*; Ia, q. 79, arts 12–13. On the sources of the concepts of *synderesis* and conscience, see E. D'Arcy, *Conscience and its Right to Freedom* (London & New York, 1961) pp. 15–19, 43–7.

94. St Thomas Aquinas, *Summa Theol.*, IaIIae, q. 94, art. ii, 3, resp. For Hobbes, see *Leviathan*, ed. W. G. Pogson Smith (Oxford, 1909; impression of 1967) ch. 14, pp. 99–100; Locke, *Essays on the Law of Nature* (Oxford, 1954) essay V, p. 172; *Second Treatise of Government* (Laslett's edn, Cambridge, 1960) sect. 135, line 31; sect. 183, lines 22–4.

95. Locke, *Essay concerning Human Understanding* (Nidditch's edn, Oxford, 1975) Bk I, ch. iii, sect. 3; *First Treatise of Government*, sect. 86, especially lines 19–23.

96. *Nic. Ethics*, Bk VIII, ch. xiii, sects 5–11; *Rhetoric*, Bk I, ch. xiii, sects 11–12.

97. Kant, *Critique of Pure Reason, Werke* (Akademie edn, Berlin, 1902 foll.; 2nd edn 1940 foll.) vol. III, p. 544. R. Bambrough has argued that a *joint* method of drawing distinctions and perceiving connections can be found in both Aristotle and Wittgenstein, and that Aristotle applied it in his discussion of justice in Book V of the *Nic. Ethics* ('Aristotle on Justice: a Paradigm in Philosophy', in *New Essays on Plato and Aristotle*, ed. R. Bambrough (London, 1965) pp. 162ff.).

98. C. J. Friedrich, *The Philosophy of Law in Historical Perspective* (Chicago, 1958) p. 24.

99. *Rhetoric*, Bk I, ch. x, sect. 3; ch. xiii, sect. 2; ch. xv, sect. 6; *Nic. Ethics*, Bk V, ch. vii.

100. *Nic. Ethics*, Bk V, ch. vi, 1134 a 26.

101. Barker, *The Politics of Aristotle*, p. 364.

102. *Nic. Ethics*, Bk V, ch. vii, 1134 b 24–7. See above, ch. 4, sect. ii, third para. from the end.
103. For a modern discussion see R. M. Hare's 'Principles', *Arist. Soc. Proc.*, LXXIII (1972–3) 1–18.
104. *Rhetoric*, Bk I, ch. i, sect. 7. See also *Politics*, Bk III, ch. xv, sect. 4; ch. xvi, sect. 11. Rousseau (*The Social Contract*, Bk II, ch. vi, paras 4–6) holds that 'there can be no general will directed to a particular object' and that 'the object of laws is always general'.
105. Cf. J. R. Lucas, 'Against Equality', *Philosophy*, XL (1965) 299–300.
106. This ultimately can be traced back to Aristotle's *Nic. Ethics*, Bk V, ch. x, 1137 b 27–9 (Locke, *Second Treatise of Government*, sects 156, 158, 159ff).
107. See *Politics*, Bk II, ch. viii, sects 21–2; Bk III, ch. xi, sects 19–21; ch. xv, sect 4; Bk IV, ch. iv, sects 30–1.
108. *Rhetoric*, Bk I, ch. xiii, sect. 19.
109. *Nic. Ethics*, Bk V, ch. x, 1137 a 31–1138 a 3. Compare J. R. Lucas, *The Principles of Politics* (Oxford, 1966; corrected repr. 1967) p. 133, n. 2: 'The just decision in a *particular case* I call equitable.'
110. See my paper 'On Justifying Inequality', *Political Studies*, XI (1963).
111. R. M. Eaton, *General Logic* (New York, 1931) pp. 343–4.
112. *Rhetoric*, Bk I, ch. xiii, sects 12–14. For *prima facie* gaps in the law and its necessary universality of scope, see J. Cohen and H. L. A. Hart, 'The Theory and Definition in Jurisprudence', *Arist. Soc.* (supp.), XXIX (1955) 227, 253–4, 258ff.
113. *Nic. Ethics*, Bk V, ch. x, 1137 b 23–4.
114. Ibid., ch. x, sects 2–6. Even in English law, the rules of Equity, though distinct from Common Law, are an important supplement to the Common Law. Again, as in Aristotle's theory, a Common Law rule may be practically, though not theoretically, nullified by a countervailing rule of Equity. See William Geldart, *Elements of English Law*, revised by Sir William Holdsworth and H. G. Hanbury (London, 1911; 4th edn 1948) ch. ii, especially pp. 21–2.
115. *Politics*, Bk III, ch. xvi, sects 5, 8, 1287 a 32, 1287 b 3–5. See *Nic. Ethics*, Bk V, ch. iv, sect. 7, 1132 a 22–4.
116. *Nic. Ethics*, Bk X, ch. ix, sect. 12.
117. Bishop Butler, *The Analogy of Religion*, pt II, ch. viii, sect. 25 (Gladstone's edn of Butler's *Works*, vol. I, p. 368).
118. *Politics*, Bk III, ch. xvi, sect. 5.
119. It is of interest to note that Wittgenstein's decided preference lay with the voluntarist theory. See F. Waismann, *Wittgenstein und der Wiener Kreis*, ed. B. F. McGuinness (Oxford, 1967) p. 115 (English translation by J. Schulte and McGuinness, Oxford, 1979), where, in an entry dated 17 December 1930, Wittgenstein writes: 'Schlick says that in theological ethics there have been two conceptions of the nature of the Good: according to the more shallow interpretation the

good is good because God wills it; according to the more profound interpretation God wills the good because it is good.' (In print, the reference is to Schlick's *Fragen der Ethik* (Vienna, 1930) p. 9; Eng. trans. *Problems of Ethics* (New York, 1939) p. 11.) 'I think that the first conception is the more profound one: good is what God commands. For it cuts off the possibility of any explanation "why" it is good, whereas the second conception is precisely the shallow, intellectualist, one, which pretends "as if" that which is good could be further justified' (my translation). One reason against the idea that goodness is what God commands is that the autonomy of ethics can be defended only on the basis of the interpretation which Wittgenstein attacks. For part of what is meant by the logical independence of ethics or by saying that moral values are absolute and not validated by authority is that they hold irrespective of what anybody (including the divine authority) either thinks or wills. Another criticism of Wittgenstein's position is that it may be held to involve the naturalistic fallacy. His defence here might have been his Protestant beliefs and his interpretation of Ockham's Razor (*Tractatus Logico-Philosophicus*, 3.328 and 5.47321). See also *Tractatus*, 6.421 and 6.5ff.

120. *Politics*, Bk VII, ch. iv, sects 7ff.
121. R. G. Collingwood, *The Idea of Nature* (Oxford, 1945) pp. 17ff. For Aristotle on happiness, see *Nic. Ethics*, Bk I, 1098 a 18–20, 1100 a 4–10, 1101 a 9–21; Bk X, 1177 b 24–5.
122. *Politics*, Bk VII, ch. iv, sect. 11.
123. For the phrase and a similar argument concerning the sovereignty of monarchical rule see St Thomas Aquinas, *De regimine principum*, Bk I, ch. ii.
124. Cf. J. Cook Wilson, *Statement and Inference* (Oxford, 1926) vol. I, p. 328.
125. H. L. A. Hart, *The Concept of Law* (Oxford, 1961) p. 181.
126. *Politics*, Bk III, ch. xiii, sects 13–14. I follow Newman (vol. III, p. 242, note on 1284 a 13) in translating the passage in question as 'there is no law *against* such persons' rather than 'concerning' or 'dealing with' such persons.
127. *Politics*, Bk IV, ch. viii, sect. 6.
128. *Rhetoric*, Bk I, ch. xv, sect. 8; cf. also ch. xiv, sect. 7.
129. For details, see Hart, *The Concept of Law*, pp. 168ff.
130. *Politics*, Bk II, ch. viii, sect. 24.
131. Sir Edward Coke, *Institutes of the Laws of England* (London, 1628) Bk IV, introductory essay.
132. For 'the precedent of antiquity', 'ancient customs', the reverence due to 'old laws', and 'the pretext of improvement', see Rousseau, *The Social Contract*, Bk III, ch. xi, last para., pp. 73–4; *A Discourse on the Origin of Inequality*, p. 147 (Everyman edn). For a modern formulation of Aristotle's distinction, see D. D. Raphael, *Justice and Liberty* (London, 1980) ch. 5.

133. *Politics*, Bk III, ch. xvi, sect. 9.
134. *Politics*, Bk V, ch. ix, sects 11–12.
135. *Politics*, Bk III, ch. xvi, sects 9–11. See above, ch. 1, sect. iv, para. 8 and n. 50.
136. *Politics*, Bk II, ch. viii, sects 16ff.
137. Benn and Peters, *Social Principles and the Democratic State* (London, 1959) p. 62.

Notes to Chapter 5: Summary and Conclusion

1. See for details my *John Locke: Essays on the Law of Nature* (Oxford, 1954) pp. 44ff.; and 'John Locke and Natural Law', *Philosophy*, XXXI (1956) 27ff.
2. Cf. Benn and Peters, *Social Principles and the Democratic State*, p. 72.
3. H. L. A. Hart, *The Concept of Law,* pp. 100, 247.
4. Locke, *Essay concerning Human Understanding*, Bk IV, ch. xxi, sect. 4.
5. *Politics*, Bk VII, ch. xiii; ch. xiv, sects 3–4, 8–11.

Notes to Appendix

1. *Metaphysics*, I, ch. v.
2. See ch. 2, sect. i, para. 4.
3. *Nic. Ethics*, Bk I, ch. vi.

Index

139